HOW TO WRITE ESSAYS

A practical guide for students

John Clanchy and Brigid Ballard

Longman Cheshire

Longman Cheshire Pty Limited
Longman House
Kings Gardens
95 Coventry Street
Melbourne 3205 Australia

Offices in Sydney, Brisbane, Adelaide and Perth,
and associated companies throughout the world.

Designed by Lauren Statham, Alice Graphics
Set in 11/12 Bembo (Linotron)
Produced by Longman Cheshire Pty Ltd
through Longman Malaysia, PP

National Library of Australia
Cataloguing-in-Publication data

Clanchy, John.
  How to write essays: a practical guide for students.

 -Bibliography.
  ISBN 0 582 87497 1.

  1. English language – Rhetoric. 2. Report writing.
  I. Ballard, Brigid. II. Title

808.042

How to Write Essays

Contents

Acknowledgements

The publishers wish to thank the following for permission to reproduce copyright material: American Psychological Association for figure 'Graph 2, At what age are we smartest?'; Harcourt Brace Jovanovich for extract from *Psychology: An Introduction*, Third edition by Jerome Kagan and Ernest Havemann © 1976 Harcourt Brace Jovanovich; New York Academy of Sciences for extract from 'Discussion Paper: The Evolution of Human Communication: what can primates tell us' by N. Tanner and A. Zihlman from *Annals of the New York Academy of Sciences*, Volume 280, 1976; Penguin Books Ltd, for extract from *Introducing Sociology*, Second edition by P. Worsley (ed.), 1970; The Psychological Corporation © 1955 for figure 'Graph 1, I.Q. by age groups'; and Faber and Faber, for extract from *The Making of Modern Ireland, 1603–1923* by J. C. Beckett, 1966.

We also wish to thank the following for extracts used: Edward Arnold for extract from *Sociolinguistics* by N. Dittmar; Cambridge University Press, U.K., for extract by A.M. Clarke and G.M. Cooper from *British Journal of Psychology*, Volume 57, 3 & 4; the Commonwealth Department of Education for extract by T. Astley from *Education News*, Volume 15, 2–3, 1975; W.H. Freeman & Co, San Francisco for extract from *Introduction to Contemporary Psychology* by E. Fantino and G.S. Reynolds; and Chatto & Windus for extract from *The Common Pursuit* by F.R. Leavis, 1952.

Preface

How to write essays is a handbook in the craft of essay writing for tertiary students and those in secondary schools who plan to continue on to tertiary studies. In it we have tried to explore the very real difficulties students face in writing academic essays. We do not offer prescriptions which ensure success nor tips on how to beat the system. We have written on the assumption, which we ourselves hold strongly, that students genuinely care about their studies, though they do sometimes become frustrated, and eventually disillusioned, if academic courses fail to offer them the intellectual satisfaction and excitement they seek. It is in this spirit that we work with our students at the Australian National University. And it is with this philosophy that we have written this book.

The approaches to essay writing which we have developed in this handbook are based on our own years of experience teaching students the strategies of reading, analysing, thinking and arguing which are appropriate to university study. In our work we are continually faced with the realization that students do want help in developing their capacities for thinking and writing. They recognize that university essay writing is a different task from writing at school. They recognize that mere rules about format and simplified advice about self-organization do not help them to grapple with the serious problems of thinking through writing. And they are right. There are no easy answers.

In teaching our own students we always try to work with current problems and genuine materials: the essays they must write, the books they must read, the notes they must take in lectures. We never treat problems and skills in isolation. They are always related to the central task of producing an essay. The approach and methods used in this book reflect our teaching practice. We have used only those materials our students and colleagues have brought to us over the years. Similarly, the production of an essay is the consistent focus of attention — it is the purpose to which all the activities of reading, thinking, arguing and writing are directed. Finally, we have emphasized continually that there is no one model for developing a successful essay. Successful essays can be very different, depending on the different demands of different disciplines, different courses, different lecturers and different topics. There may be qualities which are common to these essays, but the differences are crucial.

Above all, this book, like the process of writing which it explores, is a dialogue with the reader about the intricacies of a task which has a central role in tertiary education. It could not have been written without the assistance of all those students who, over the years, have participated in our courses or sought our advice about writing and, in particular, those students and staff who have spent time and energy reading and commenting upon successive drafts of this book. We are grateful to them and hope they will feel that their time was well spent.

John Clanchy
Brigid Ballard

Australian National University
Canberra

Introduction

This book is designed to help you develop, in a practical way, your own capacities for essay writing. It will not be of much assistance if you are looking for:

- short cuts or tips or easy solutions to writing problems,
- a formula approach which can be applied to every essay you write,
- advice on how to beat the system.

If you hope to find 'instant answers' in this book, you will be disappointed. However, if you want guidance in the difficult tasks of:

- analysing a topic,
- reading for ideas and information,
- taking notes for an essay,
- developing a structure for your ideas,
- expressing those ideas clearly and fluently,
- editing your essay to meet academic criteria of correctness,

then your concerns coincide with our own.

We have based all our explanations on actual examples and materials drawn from the experience of our own students. The essay topics, the readings, the examples of student writing are all genuine.

How you use this handbook is your own affair. Throughout it we insist that there is no one 'right' way of working through any stage of the process of writing an essay. And there is no 'right' way of using this book. But, as with essay writing, there are ways which are probably more fruitful than others. We suggest that you:

- merely glance through the book, first time around, just to get some idea of what is covered. Do this before you decide to buy it; check that it is directed towards at least some of your own concerns.

- use it, or the sections of it relevant to your own problems, when you are *in the process* of writing an essay.
- after you get an essay back, read those sections of the book which relate to points criticized in your essay by your lecturer.

In other words, try to use the advice given in this book in its proper context. Advice received out of context is never much use; handbooks on essay writing seldom make fascinating reading in isolation. But when you are actually in the throes of producing an essay, you may find this book is genuinely useful.

Clearing the ground

Why write essays?

In the modern world our thinking is largely transmitted by speech and through radio and television. At the university, however, you are required to do much of your thinking through writing. In the Humanities and Social Sciences you are inevitably required to produce a considerable number of formal essays. You may also have to respond to multiple-choice or short answer tests, write brief reports or short reviews and criticisms. But most of your more important writing will be in the form of extended essays. It will involve a commitment on your part of time, energy and mental effort. As you will soon find out for yourself, essay writing is hard work — and it doesn't get very much easier as you advance in your studies.

While this may seem a depressing outlook, it is realistic. Certainly you will, with time and experience, become more proficient in such skills as interpreting topics, handling research and sources, and mastering academic language and presentation. But the central intellectual struggle to shape your thoughts into written words and to connect those thoughts into a coherent argument will remain as demanding as it seemed when you were faced with your first essay assignment.

Yet write essays you must. There are usually compelling *external* pressures for their production: they are used to assess your progress; they are an integral part of academic teaching. There are also equally important *personal* reasons for committing your ideas to writing. E.M. Forster once asked: 'How the devil do I know what I think till I see what I've written?', and it is, after all, to develop your thinking in new areas and to new purposes that you have come to university. It is by writing, even more than by speech, that you actually master your material and extend your own understanding. Writing enables you to build ideas systematically one upon another; and to do so over an extended period with opportunities to pause and reflect along the way. Writing is nearly always a struggle; but it can also be immensely satisfying.

False leads and folk tales

One of the hazards you will soon encounter in your efforts to find out what is expected of you in an essay is the misleading advice of fellow students. You will be told blithely, 'Oh, the best way to write an essay is to stay up all night and just toss it off without thinking too much about it'. Another version of this folk tale is that you should just 'rave on', using as much of the jargon and clichés of the subject as you can remember and preferably including material which caters for the known interests of the marker. Such advice is unsound. It may occasionally be possible to write some essays on the basis of a quick response and you may also meet occasional academics who strongly favour certain approaches to a topic. But, as a long-term working rule, essays which will satisfy both your reader and, more importantly, yourself, take a considerable period of thinking, writing and rewriting. So it would be wise to treat such advice with scepticism.

Another common folk tale is that there is a specific 'skill' or 'knack' involved in writing a successful essay and that if only you can improve your 'technique' or discover this magic 'skill', all will fall into place. Alas, not so. Certainly there are strategies for approaching your topic, strategies for thinking about and researching your material, strategies for the more effective organisation of your argument, and simple skills in the presentation of the final draft. But there is no *one* set of skills which can guarantee success. Just as there is no one perfect essay. And no one perfect answer for any topic. Each essay is, in T.S. Eliot's words, 'a raid on the inarticulate'.

Students are not the only source of well-intended misdirection about writing academic essays. You may find that some of your lecturers and tutors mislead you with superficial comments about the ease of the exercise they have set. They may encourage you by assuring you that 'all you need do is just answer the topic which is set; keep to the point and develop your own clear argument'. How true — but how difficult. You will be told: 'I'll accept any reasonable point of view and any evidence so long as it is logical and sound'. But how are you to recognise 'sound evidence'? And how are you to know what limits the lecturer sets on 'reasonable' in relation to the discipline and to the set topic?

Another common piece of advice is that all you have to do is make sure your essay has 'a beginning, a middle and an end'. This is indisputably good advice; but how to begin, what should come in the middle, and where it should all end, is the real problem.

What then can be done? Where can you start your apprenticeship in academic writing and thinking?

A good place to start might be to find out what your lecturer really expects you to produce in your essay.

General assumptions about your approach to writing

Your lecturers assume that your essay will be a *serious* piece of writing and that it will merit close reading. They assume that you have spent a considerable proportion of time in each stage of the production of your essay: in the reading and research; in selecting and ordering your materials and ideas; in writing and rewriting drafts of the essay; and in the final editing and presentation. It is true that the amount of time you spend on an essay does not in itself ensure success. Especially at the start of your university studies, you may find you are working inefficiently — maybe spending too much time on reading only marginally relevant books; maybe taking inadequate notes so that you have to refer back to the source materials a second time for specific facts and references; maybe rewriting and getting blocked on one section of the essay.

Your lecturers also assume that you will be able to comprehend the necessary sources. You will earn credit not for the mere comprehension of these materials but for the way in which you use them in constructing your argument. It is not sufficient to merely summarise the books and articles you have read, or to string together a series of well-chosen quotations and paraphrases from these sources. Nor is it enough to merely describe or narrate what happened during a certain period of history or in a certain novel or play. You are expected to know all this groundwork and then to use this knowledge in order to construct an argument based on the set topic. A common academic comment on an essay which has merely 'covered the ground' is: 'I can see you have read widely and put a lot of effort into your work *but* there is no analysis . . .' or, more bluntly, 'So what?'

Specific expectations about your essay

What makes a 'good' essay? Analysis of comments on students' essays suggests that there are four major areas of performance about which academics hold clear expectations.

In the rest of this chapter we attempt to clarify these four expectations. You will notice that in each case we follow the same pattern: first, we define the expectation; second, we explain what it means in practice; finally, we present a selection of academics' comments relating to it. These comments are taken from a range of student essays.

Relevance to set topic

It is expected that your essay will be clearly focused on the set topic and will deal fully with its central concerns.

In most undergraduate courses the lecturer sets the topics for essay assignments. Whatever the course and whatever the wording of the topic, the lecturer will probably have at least three objectives he or she wants to develop:

1 your understanding of a general theme, concept or area of material. For example, a Political Science lecturer will set an essay focused on the nature of 'bureaucracy'.

2 your capacity to handle this general concept for a particular purpose. For example, the Political Science essay topic may start:

Is it fair to argue that Cabinet Ministers are controlled by their departments?

3 your ability to relate general theory to specific examples. For example, the full form of the Political Science assignment:

> Is it fair to argue that Cabinet Ministers are controlled by their departments? Discuss in the light of either the British or the Australian experience in the last ten years.

In all essay assignments you are required to read and think your way towards a considered judgement about a complex matter. You may be required to use both original materials (primary sources) and other writers' interpretations of these materials (secondary sources). The first should provide the basis for your thinking. The second may suggest starting points for critical analysis.

In practice you will be expected to:

1 recognise the assumptions and implications underlying the actual wording of the topic and take account of them in the course of your essay.

2 handle the topic and its key terms within the limits of the course and discipline being studied. (This can be a complex matter as it requires you to distinguish clearly between different uses of the same terms. For example, consider the ways in which you would need to interpret the term 'development' in Economics and Psychology essay topics.)

3 focus consistently on the key ideas and terms throughout your essay.

4 cover all the parts of the set topic. Some topics will include a number of sub-topics or sub-questions related to the main theme.

Lecturers' comments

> Good work. You've covered the topic well and put much thought into your essay.

> The second major fault in the essay is that far too much of it is not immediately relevant to the topic you chose. The task before you was quite specific and clear. Instead of tackling that task directly and without delay, you discourse at large around the topic for page after page. Even your discussion of Y is not made relevant to the central question of X. Why not go directly to your evidence, especially the evidence of the debates themselves (of

which you make very limited use), asking yourself 'What does this tell me in answer to the question before me?'

I can see that you have done some reading for this essay and understand the broad outlines of the subject, but this is not really a satisfactory essay. It is *much* too general. There are two questions to be answered and they are both very specific. You spend at least half the essay on other matters — such as why wheeled transport developed, or how it was used, or the role of chariots in war, and so on. Much of the first two pages are not even vaguely relevant. This leaves you very little room to discuss the second part of the question. What you must aim for is a tight account of a very limited topic, anchored directly to specific pieces of evidence.

This is a perfectly reasonable essay but, unfortunately, rather off the track. The question asked for a discussion of the role of the *relationship* of X to Y, not of Y per se. There is certainly some overlap and you have, in an implicit way, touched on some of the issues pertinent to the topic, but in all of this you have not really dealt to any satisfactory degree with the X relationship. Did you misread the essay topic?

This essay is all over the place. You start off talking about 'society' as aggregates of human beings, i.e. talking sociologically, and end up using the word to mean something like 'high society' or a collection of aunts in Jane Austen's drawing-room.

Well researched and well presented. At times you wandered a little from the point but your argument was generally quite clear.

Use made of written sources

It is expected that your essay will be the result of wide and critical reading.

For most topics on which you are asked to write at university you will find that there is more reading available than you can possibly get through. In secondary school your courses of study were usually based on a core textbook. You knew that if you mastered what was in that textbook you could be confident that you had covered the material of the course. This principle does not hold true at university. Even in those courses for which there is a core text, it is assumed that you will also read widely around the topics set for tutorials and essays. No single book or journal article will cover the material you now need to handle your assignments adequately. (Essays in literary criticism, which often focus on a single text, may be exceptions to this general rule. Therefore you will need to make the reservation 'But that's not necessarily true for literature essays' about some suggestions made in this discussion.)

In many courses you will be given a preliminary list of books and articles. The references and bibliographies in these readings will lead you to further sources — and yet further references. So you must develop the capacity to read selectively and critically.

In practice you will be expected to:

1 read with a questioning mind. Do not accept that something is true simply because it is published. Do not expect that there is any single correct answer to complex questions.

2 read in order to understand both the meaning of each individual sentence and its relationship to the developing structure of the argument.

3 evaluate continuously what you are reading. First, you will need to test the opinions and judgements of the writer against the evidence he or she provides, and against the opinions and judgements of other writers — and maybe against your own experience. Second, you must decide whether this material is relevant to the purposes of your essay.

Lecturers' comments

We are not interested in your opinion but in well-founded argument based on wide reading.

Your reading has been nowhere near wide enough. You have merely presented a précis of some of the arguments of a couple of writers. The references you have made to X appear as if they were put in because a handout said you ought to read that if you are doing the topic. Nowhere is there any attempt to present an alternative view... Quite simply, this essay is much too superficial to meet the requirements of a university course.

This is a thoughtfully argued essay based on wide reading and imaginative research.

Well done. Based on extensive and intensive research, and giving an independent response.

Much of this essay is simply variations on the same theme. X says this; others agree; therefore it must be correct.

What you say is all very well, but it is only *one* view. It happens to be the one I share but there is little evidence in this essay that you are aware of the objections which some writers have raised to it, or of some of the problems it raises.

The secondary sources are intended to supplement the primary sources and guide you in your reading. They should be read judiciously and not treated as authoritative. Nobody's opinions (even the lecturer's) are more valid than the sources on which they are based.

I suspect that the main reason why your essay is misdirected is that instead of setting your own objectives and pursuing them by your own examination of relevant evidence, you have allowed your own ideas and objectives to be dictated by the historians you have read. Since their questions are not identical with yours, by following them you were led away from your proper objectives. You have obviously worked hard at reading your secondary sources. The same amount of work put into an analysis of thoroughly relevant primary sources would have paid better dividends. Try to have the confidence to do your own thing in your own way, using secondary sources as critics of your ideas, stimuli to those ideas and sources of information, rather than as guides to (or even substitutes for) the ideas you should have.

A reasoned argument

It is expected that your essay will present a reasoned argument.

In the course of your reading and research for an essay you will collect a substantial amount of material. Facts, ideas, opinions, definitions, quantitative data, quotations, etc. — these become the raw material on which your thinking and your essay are based. They have little significance in themselves. They only assume significance when you use them to develop a systematic point of view or argument.

The term *argument* is used in a special sense in relation to academic essays. It does not mean that you must necessarily 'take sides' or present only one point of view. Rather it means that you explore the topic through a clear and consistent development of ideas, using adequate evidence. So your lecturer will expect your key terms and concepts to be defined, if they are complex, and your general statements to be supported by evidence drawn from relevant sources. He or she will also expect the organisation of your material to be directed towards the conclusion you wish to draw.

In practice you will be expected to:

1 select only points which are directly relevant to your topic and your argument, discarding those which may have seemed relevant when your ideas were still developing.

2 structure the material so that the main ideas are presented logically and coherently, i.e. each idea must fit reasonably with that which precedes it and that which follows, and the ideas taken together must lead consistently to your overall conclusion.

3 ensure that each section of your argument is internally consistent, with the evidence, examples, and quotations clearly supporting or extending the central idea being developed.

4 take into account alternative points of view or interpretations of the materials you have used.

Lecturers' comments

You fail to make connections between your descriptive examples and your general points.

You have some real points, but your arrangement of them is disorderly.

Where is the thread on this page—in fact in this essay?

The main problem with this essay is linking the discussion in each section to the main theme. In general the examples you give are relevant to the five points raised by X. However, you cover so many social situations that it is hard to see any consistent thread in each section and impossible to find one in the essay as a whole. You should try to concentrate on a particular issue...to focus your theoretical ideas.

This appears to be a mish-mash of facts, assembled for no obvious purpose... In effect this is not your work but that of the various authors you have photocopied. You have not developed an argument from the material. In future, organise your thoughts: think what the whole essay title means, and how the relevant facts fit together and in what order, to provide an answer to the problem.

There are some interesting observations here but nowhere do they add up to a case.

In writing your next essay, remember that you are arguing a case. No one is going to be persuaded to accept that case unless it is built solidly on adequate evidence: not on 'reasonable' assertions, assumptions or suggestions. Remember too, that you will have a quite specific task to perform; and concentrate your energies on *that* task, resisting all temptations to be drawn aside into byways, however interesting in themselves.

Presentation

It is expected that your essay will be competently presented.

In the final version of the essay you need to pay attention to the formal presentation of your material. There are two levels at which your lecturer expects the presentation to be competent:

1 the surface level of grammar, spelling, handwriting or typing, referencing, and use of quotations, etc.

2 the appropriateness of your writing style to the task.

In practice you will be expected to:

1 adopt a tone and style which are appropriate to academic writing in general and to the special demands of the discipline in which you are working;

2 use the necessary specialist terminology accurately;

3 use the correct format for quotations;

4 follow the form of referencing and bibliographic citation which is standard for the discipline;

5 present graphic and numerical data accurately and economically;

6 edit your essay carefully for errors in grammar, spelling and punctuation, and for precision in choice of words and expression of ideas.

Lecturers' comments

What you say may be reasonable enough but the way in which you say it is simply inadequate. Your essay is full of vague, awkward and misconstructed sentences. I'm afraid that you won't pass this subject until you learn to express yourself more clearly and precisely.

Your expression is sometimes extremely awkward to the extent that the thought you are attempting to convey becomes obscured or mangled.

Stylistically and organisationally, this is much too incoherent to pass. Your problems with expression are serious. Too many of your sentences are grammatical fragments, like quickly jotted notes rather than complete units. And you haven't organised your material effectively. Paragraphs seems to be conglomerations of only vaguely related ideas, not logically unified series of sentences... The raw material for a better essay is apparent. But it is unshaped, and the shaping process (i.e. organisation and expression) is an essential aspect of logical and critical thinking.

You tend to use words and ideas rather loosely, without being precise enough about what you mean.

Write in whole sentences, not stock phrases: take care with your spelling and your style of writing.

This is a very impressive piece of *research* and a rather indifferent piece of *reporting*. Your writing is often obscure, clumsy and wordy. I don't feel sure how 'I should mark this but on balance I think I should give high marks for what you have discovered and a severe reprimand for your bad language.

For the future, how about using *our* footnoting style?

Bibliography and footnotes are excellent. Apart from a few minor slips, you use scholarly apparatus well and it is gratifying to find a student who gives it careful treatment.

You do at times reach for real insights here, but you do them less than justice. Your expression is very often repetitive, loose and inept. Your sentences could often be shortened without loss of sense, with a gain in precision.

Summary

In this chapter we have attempted to clear away a few misconceptions about ways of writing essays. We have also looked at some of the qualities which lecturers expect in a good essay.

The main points to remember are:

1 Your essay should be relevant to the set topic in both content and focus.

2 You should read widely and critically in order to accumulate and select your material.

3 You should present a reasoned argument, based on valid evidence and leading to a clear conclusion.

4 Your lecturer will be looking not only at the material you have selected but, more importantly, at the use you have made of it.

5 You should aim at precision, accuracy, and appropriateness in language, style and format.

6 There is no single set of skills or techniques which will ensure that you produce a satisfactory essay.

2

Choosing the essay topic

Having cleared away some of the folk tales and misconceptions about writing university essays, you can now begin the process of producing an essay. It all starts with the list of essay topics handed out by your lecturer. You must now decide which topic you are going to commit yourself to reading, thinking and writing about during the next few days or weeks. Since so much of your energy and interest will be invested in your essay, to say nothing of the assessment value attached to the final product, it is important to choose your topic carefully.

When you first look at the list of set topics you may only be separating those questions which immediately attract you from those which do not. You will probably do this initial sorting on the basis of the *content* of the questions: do I want to work on Hamlet or The Alchemist? on ritual or kinship? on licensing systems or the gold standard? But this is only part of the task facing you. This content is governed by the special purpose and emphasis of the essay topic. Are you being asked to use your knowledge of Hamlet to explore the nature of dramatic tragedy? or the effectiveness of Hamlet's soliloquies in the development of plot and character? or the role of minor characters in the creation of dramatic tension?

Your lecturers have worded your essay topics with care. They know what ideas and what content they want you to cover in your reading and your thinking about the topic. They may also point out the way in which they expect you to develop your material. This does not mean, however, that there is only one 'right' way of answering the question. What it does mean is that there are limits on the ways you can handle it. Therefore you should, from the very outset, take time to analyse what it is that the lecturer probably wants. This can save you from labouring over an essay only to have it criticized as 'irrelevant' or 'wandering from the point' or 'only answering part of the set question'. This approach will also enable you to read and research more effectively and to take better notes. In this way you start with a least a tentative purpose which you will be able to refine as you find out more about the subject.

Characteristics of academic essays

Most essays in the Humanities and Social Sciences share certain general characteristics. First, you will seldom be asked merely to *explain* or to *describe* a process or event, although this would be a common demand for a school essay. Now the task is more complex. You are nearly always required to combine description with *analysis*. For example, look at this History topic:

> From Cobbett's Parliamentary History, Cobbett's Parliamentary Debates or Hansard's Parliamentary Debates, choose any one debate on any one day (1760–1850) on any issue. Identify the speakers and discuss the issues and attitudes revealed in that particular debate.

Would a summary of the debate satisfy all the demands made in this topic?

Second, you will find that all your essays require you to relate *general* concepts, ideas and theories to *particular* materials or, conversely, to move from specific events and instances to a more general interpretation of their significance. For example, consider these topics:

> Laughter can range from innocent delight to cruel mockery. How would you describe the nature of the comedy in either Twelfth Night or The Alchemist?

> Can the life of the water buffalo in central Java be described as a clear case of symbiosis between man and animal?

It is the *significant relationship* between the general and the particular which the lecturer is directing you to explore in such topics.

Third, you will find that most essays require you to gather ideas and information from printed sources rather than to draw on your own experience. This too may be a contrast to your school essay writing.

Finally, nearly all your essay topics will involve materials which can be interpreted in more than one way; thus there will be a problem or controversy which you must analyse and attempt to resolve. It is unlikely that there will be any one, or only one, 'correct' answer or interpretation. For example, look at this Linguistics topic:

> If you had to devise a new artificial language, which could be learnt 'easily', which word classes and which syntactic relations would you consider as absolutely indispensable?

and this Philosophy essay:

> Masters or servants. Which are the freer?

Clearly you are not expected to explain definitively the nature of freedom or to develop a total language system. Rather you are being asked to consider various aspects of a problem, select the approach which seems to you most satisfactory, and develop it according to suitable criteria.

Immediate concerns

What do you think about first when choosing an essay topic? Probably, content, what has to be done with it (the intellectual demands), and some more practical matters such as limitations of time and availability of books.

What is the essay about?

There are a number of different aspects to this question. *First*, you need to check the general area of *content* defined by key words in the topic. Thus,

> To what extent does environment affect Australian Aboriginal organization and demography?

is an essay about the Australian environment and about Aborigines, and it is not about Alaska or the Eskimo (though you might, in passing, wish to compare them).
  Similarly,

> 'The poem records a vital change or development of awareness; by the end, he (the poet) has reached a state of mind and/or feeling which subtly differs from that of his opening lines.'

> Discuss any two of Donne's poems, explaining why and how far (if at all) you think this true of each.

is a question about the poetry of John Donne, and not another poet, and about the development of states of mental or emotional awareness in two poems, and not about the relation between Donne's poetry and the intellectual movements of his day.

What is the general area of content in this Economics essay?

Analyse the causes and effects of a shift in the savings-national income schedule.

Second, you should identify the specific concepts on which the topic is focused. The Anthropology essay is about the relationship which exists between three concepts: environment (not ritual), social organization (not economic, though the two may be related) and demography. What concepts can you identify in the Donne essay?

Third, you are asked for *judgement*. In the light of your knowledge and reading, how far can something be said to be true? 'To what extent ...' implies that there may be at least some truth in the relationship suggested. '... why and how far (if at all) you think this true ...' even allows room for denying the whole basis of the original quotation. It is clear that in each essay there is room for considerable difference in judgement.

Fourth, you should be aware that the essays are 'about' different bodies of knowledge or *disciplines*. The first is 'about' Anthropology; the second is 'about' literary criticism. Different disciplines ask different questions. Thus some questions which are relevant and should be asked in Anthropology are judged irrelevant to literary criticism. For example, the topic 'Aboriginal folklore' would lead an anthropologist to questions about Aboriginal culture and ways of seeing the world. A literary critic would want to consider its quality as a work of art.

Once you have decided what each essay on your list is about, you can pick out those topics which seem interesting. But are they manageable?

What are the practical considerations?

At this stage of choosing your topic many other considerations will begin to flood in upon you. How long must the essay be? When is it due? Does a topic overlap or complement an essay you have already decided to do in another course? Is it advisable to work on closely related topics, or would it seem better to choose something completely different? Is it advisable to try and balance types of essays, e.g. one requiring extensive reading with one involving close interpretation of only one or two sources? Have your tutor, lecturer or friends discussed the advantages or disadvantages of any particular topic? What about the availability of books and other source materials? Does any topic seem more obviously straightforward or more clearly defined and limited than others? Do some require you to start from almost total ignorance, while others can be developed from material already covered? Is one intriguing? Or boring? If your lecturer is a specialist in the United States Reconstruction era or in visual perception theory, would it be advisable to select or avoid an essay focused on this area?

There are no certain answers to such questions. They all depend on your own situation, interests and judgement. By considering them, however, you should be able to identify those essays which, for you, seem to be the more manageable. You will then be in a position to choose the topic which both reflects your own interests and can be managed within the limits imposed by time and other commitments.

Making up your own topic

You may, on occasion, be permitted to make up your own essay topic, particularly in the second and later years of your course when you are beginning to write essays involving extensive research. This option, however, brings its own problems. You may find that the major difficulty occurs in actually defining and wording your topic. You should not expect that you will be able to settle on a precise topic immediately. You will need to read extensively and to talk with your tutor or essay supervisor before you can narrow down your general interest in some subject to a specifically manageable focus for an essay. If you do not maintain close contact with your tutor or supervisor during this period, you may find that you have set yourself an 'unanswerable' question or one for which there are inadequate resources available in the library.

Here is the advice one lecturer gave in a handout to students in a History course:

Do not expect at this stage that you can specify your subject in detail. Defining the subject is a process which continues as you work on it and gradually decide exactly what directions you are going to take with it.

Usually you will reduce your original coverage as you move into the chosen field. The research essay is a study in depth which cannot cover too much ground if the results are to be significant. A student could begin, for example, with an interest in trade unions and their links with political parties and finish with an essay on the declared attitudes (not actions) of the Labour Party (not all political parties) expressed in Parliament (not elsewhere) between 1900 and 1945.

This narrowing of focus can be graphically represented as an inverted pyramid. Set out below are four of the many stages a first-year European History student went through in developing a manageable focus for her essay.

Initial general interest

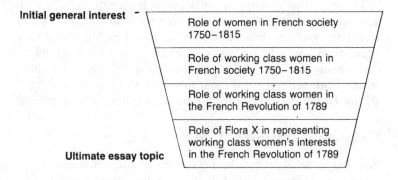

Role of women in French society 1750–1815

Role of working class women in French society 1750–1815

Role of working class women in the French Revolution of 1789

Role of Flora X in representing working class women's interests in the French Revolution of 1789

Ultimate essay topic

Summary

In this chapter we have looked at the processes involved in the selection of an essay topic. We have also touched on some of the initial stages of analysis of topics. (The job of analysis is dealt with, in greater detail, in Chapter 5.)

The important points to remember are:

1 You need to give time and thought to the interpretation and selection of the topic on which you will write.

2 Your topic will almost invariably involve analysis as well as explanation or description and will require you to relate general concepts to particular materials or events.

3 You will be confronted with problems or controversies for which there is no single 'solution' or explanation and asked to make critical judgements amongst competing solutions or explanations.

4 When you are considering what an essay is 'about', you should take into account the area of content defined by your topic, the specific concepts involved, the suggested relationships amongst those concepts and the discipline within which you are working.

5 Your choice of topic will also be partly conditioned by practical considerations of time, availability of sources, and other commitments.

6 If you are creating your own topic, you must consult closely with your tutor or supervisor to ensure that the topic is manageable.

3

Reading for your essay

Let us suppose, then, that you have chosen your essay topic and you are now ready to begin your reading. Where can you start?

Resources: what should you read?

There are at least three starting points: advice from your lecturer or tutor or from other students; your notes from lectures and tutorials; and reading lists provided in the course.

Advice from academics and students

Sometimes you may find that your lecturer or tutor is prepared to discuss the essay topic with you at the very outset. He or she may suggest a suitable introductory text-book or a journal article which covers the most recent research in the field. More often staff prefer to discuss your topic with you *after* you have done some initial reading. By that stage you will be more aware of the crucial issues involved and of the difficulties in finding relevant information.

Other students are often a useful source of information about relevant books. The recommendations of students who have already worked their way through the same or a related essay topic are valuable because they are based on experience.

Notes from lectures and tutorial discussions

Your lectures and tutorials may touch on some issues related to your essay topic. In such cases your notes should provide you with clues about where to begin your reading, and which writers and journals are most authoritative. However, lectures and tutorials will seldom cover the material with the same focus as that required in your essay. So your notes can only be a starting point. In fact lecturers often deliberately set essay topics on content that has not been covered in the formal course. Thus you are expected to develop the material independently through your own reading.

Reading lists

You may be given a general reading list for each course and a specific reading list for each essay. Such lists can provide an excellent starting point for your reading. However, you need to keep two points in mind:

1 It may be neither necessary nor useful to try to read all the suggested materials.

2 You may need to read other books and articles not on the list.

How should reading lists be used? Look at the following topic and suggested readings which were given to students in a Prehistory course. Even if you know nothing about Prehistory, you can recognise how such a list can be used effectively.

Topic: What light do you think can be shed on the early stages of human behaviour by the study of non-human primates?

Reading list:
De Vore, I. (ed.) (1965), Primate Behaviour, Holt, Rinehart & Winston (esp. chapters by Goodall & Schaller).
Goodall, J. (1971), In the Shadow of Man, Collins.
Itani, J. & Suzuki, A. (1967), 'The social unit of chimpanzees', Primates, 8, pp. 335–81.
Kortlandt, A. (1972), New Perspectives on Ape and Human Evolution, Stichting voor Psychobiologie, Amsterdam.
Napier, J.R. (1971), The Roots of Mankind, Allen & Unwin.
Oakley, K.P. (1959), 'Tools makyth man', Antiquity, 31, pp. 199–209.
_____ (1969), 'Man the skilled toolmaker' Antiquity, 43, pp. 222–3.
Reynolds, V. (1966), 'Open groups in hominid evolution', Man, ns 1, pp. 441–52.
Suzuki, A. (1967), 'An ecological study of chimpanzees in savannah woodland', Primates, 10, pp. 335–81.
Wright, R.V.S. (1972), 'Imitative learning of a flaked stone technology—The case of an orangutan', Mankind, 8, pp. 296–306.

What can you learn from the reading list?

You can start by linking the list back to the essay topic. What is the content of this essay topic?

- the behaviour of early man
- the behaviour of non-human primates

What might be involved in answering the question?

- a survey of the known behaviour of early man and of significant studies of non-human primate behaviour
- a comparison of these surveys in order to evaluate how far the study of non-human primates does throw light on the study of human behaviour
- your own conclusions on the advantages and limitations of this comparative approach, based on the evidence you have presented.

How does the reading list help to clarify your understanding of the topic?

A quick look at the titles of the books (underlined) and articles (in inverted commas) suggests that there are:

- two fairly general books (Kortlandt, Napier)
- two books specifically on primates (De Vore, Goodall)
- three articles on group or social organisation among hominids and chimpanzees (Itani & Suzuki, Reynolds, Suzuki)
- three articles on toolmaking (Oakley, Wright).

So now you can recognise that there are at least these two areas — social organisation and toolmaking — in which researchers have attempted to compare primate behaviour and early human behaviour. And therefore your essay will probably need to cover at least these two areas.

Which text should you start with?

The earliest? The shortest? Or, in a practical world, the first one you find still available on the library shelf? Assuming that you do have some choice, it is probably best to begin with the *most recent general survey* of the topic, unless you know that an earlier book is the standard work in the field. In the Prehistory example you would probably start with the Kortlandt book which is the most recent book on the list. The title, New Perspectives ..., suggests that it should include a survey of current research. Also, the chances are good that the bibliography and footnote references will direct you to other relevant readings.

Alternatively you may find that a recent journal article would be a better starting point. A book is often the concluding point of an investigation by the writer, and may well be out of date by the time it reaches print. If your topic focuses on an area of recent controversy or on the understanding of new materials, then journal articles are frequently more useful sources than books. On the other hand, scholarly controversy can be confusing if you are new to a discipline. You can sometimes feel, as you read an article, that you are overhearing a heated argument which started long ago and about which you lack sufficient background to make sense of the current debate.

In any case you will probably begin with a recent general treatment of the topic and then progress to more detailed readings on specific areas. The amount that you read and the extent to which you pursue the details will depend on the demands of your essay assignment. Is it a 2000 word or a 5000 word essay? Are you expected to produce it within three weeks or three months? How much time, energy and interest are you prepared to devote to the task?

If you want to try out your skill in interpreting another essay topic and reading list, turn to Appendix 1

If there is no reading list provided for your course or topic, then you must fall back on your own capacity to use the library facilities, card catalogues, accumulative indexes to journals, and the advice of library staff. The same principles of selection still apply: start with a recent *general* survey and then extend your reading through the references and bibliographies in the books and articles you have found useful.

Once you start your reading, however, you will be faced with a new set of problems:

- there is too much to read — 'I never have enough time to get through it all.'
- the materials are difficult to understand — 'It seems to go in one eye and out the other. I just can't concentrate on it.'
- it is hard to select material from the readings — 'How do I know what I'll need for my essay?'

Reading strategies: how should you read?

There are various strategies for reading which, it is claimed, will help you overcome these problems. Three of the most commonly suggested techniques are:

1 **Speed reading**, which attempts to solve only your first problem — lack of time — but does little to solve the problems of comprehension and selection. This technique is more suited to general reading than to academic study.

2 **SQ3R**, which is a method developed to increase the reader's power of comprehension. It was designed for school level reading and does little to help you handle the time constraints and need for selective reading at university.

3 **Scanning by key words and phrases**, which is useful for identifying isolated pieces of information but ignores the need for close attention which is essential in following a complex argument.

One strategy, however, is appropriate to academic reading.

Skimming by paragraphs

This technique makes systematic use of the structure of thought within a passage. In most academic writing the paragraph is an *idea unit*, coherent in itself and also contributing to the logical continuity of the whole argument. Another important feature of good academic writing is *clear signposting* of both the internal connections and the overall development of ideas. These signposts may be individual words and phrases, such as 'However', 'On the other hand' or 'Finally', or key sentences which state the topic being developed. They commonly occur at the start of a paragraph and it is this characteristic of style which makes skimming possible.

By glancing only at the *opening sentence of each paragraph* you can very frequently pick up an understanding of the outline of the argument being presented. Try out this technique yourself on the following chapter from a standard work on Irish history — The Making of Modern Ireland, 1603–1923, by J.C. Beckett. Before you begin to read the chapter, turn to page 38 for instructions on the steps to be followed.

Chapter Seventeen
The Great Famine

(1)

The famine of 1845–9 is a major dividing-line in the history of modern Ireland. Politically, economically and socially, the period that followed it appears sharply distinct from the period that preceded it. In some ways this appearance is misleading: one effect of the famine was to concentrate in a few brief years changes that would otherwise have been spread over genera-tions, and thus to disguise the real continuity between the two periods. But the very rapidity of these changes affected their character; and the immense burden of human suffering by which they were accompanied left an indelible mark on the popular memory. The historical importance of the Great Famine lies not only in the physical results that followed from it—the decline in population, the transfer of property, the changes in agriculture —but in the attitude to the government and to the ruling class that it engendered in the great majority of the people.

From one point of view, there was nothing exceptional about the Great Famine save its extent and its intensity. Every year, a large section of the population was, for a period of two or three months, practically destitute; and on several occasions during the earlier nineteenth century, notably in 1817 and 1822, this destitution had amounted to absolute famine in some parts of the country. This state of affairs seemed to be the inevitable result of social and economic conditions. Ireland in the 1840s, with over 8 000 000 inhabitants, of whom more than four-fifths lived on the land, was one of the most densely populated coun-tries in Europe. Even in some rural areas the population was as high as 400 per square mile, and over the country as a whole it averaged 335 per square mile of arable land. About half this population depended for its subsistence on the potato, and it was local and partial failures of the potato crop that had produced the earlier famines. What gave its special character to the Great Famine was that the crop failed over the whole country, and that the failure was repeated in successive years.

Though the dangers inherent in the Irish situation had long been recognised, no government had proved capable of working out any means of ameliorating it; and with the increase of population the margin of safety, always precarious, had grown narrower. Yet no one had foreseen a catastrophe such as actually occurred; and the very fact that there had been earlier potato failures and earlier famines made it natural to suppose, at first, that this was no more than a repetition of a familiar phenomenon. When the 'blight' on the potato crop was first reported, from the south of England, in August 1845, a few people quickly realised that if it should spread to Ireland its effect on the whole country would be infinitely more disastrous than in Great Britain; but even when the blight did appear in Ireland, in the following month, there was considerable divergence of view about its significance. And for a time this divergence was sustained by conflicting reports: some areas had escaped the blight altogether, and in others its effect was not immediately apparent—the potatoes seemed perfectly healthy when dug, only to putrefy later on.

Difference of opinion about the seriousness of the potato failure did not arise solely from variation in the reports; there was a political reason also. For some years Peel had been moving slowly towards the belief that the corn laws ought to be repealed, and events in Ireland convinced him that he must act at once. For the irreconcilable protectionists, who comprised a great part of Peel's own party, it was, therefore, a matter of policy to minimise the danger of famine. They seized on every favourable report, they declared that the others were exaggerated, and they discouraged the preparation of relief schemes as unnecessary. It was a misfortune for Ireland that the reality of the famine should have become a political question, and that the preparation of remedial measures should have become entangled in one of the bitterest parliamentary conflicts of the nineteenth century.

It is to Peel's credit that he did not allow personal or party interests to interfere with his plans for relief. Early in November 1845 he arranged, on his own responsibility, for the purchase by the government of £100 000's worth of Indian corn in the United States, and for its shipment to Cork. It was not his intention that the government should undertake responsibility for feeding the people; but he believed that by selling this grain cheaply it would be possible to keep down the general price of food, and prevent profiteering. He placed his main reliance, however, on local efforts by the gentry and professional classes; and a relief commission set up by the government in November had, as its first main task, the organisation of local committees, which were to raise funds and distribute food. At the same time, the board of works was to undertake the construction of new roads, a traditional method of providing employment in hard seasons.

Though Peel took the initiative in these measures, their direction fell largely into the hands of Charles Trevelyan, assistant secretary to the treasury, and one of the new generation that was transforming the character of the British civil service. Trevelyan worked day and night at his task; but his outlook was dominated by the prevailing *laissez-faire* philosophy, and at times he gave the impression that he was more alarmed lest the Irish should be demoralised by receiving too much help from the government than lest they should die of starvation through not receiving enough. 'You cannot', one of his agents in Ireland reminded him, 'answer the cry of want by a quotation from political economy';

but the warning had little effect. Nevertheless, during the first season of famine, from the autumn of 1845 to the summer of 1846, the government's measures were substantially successful. And this success was due mainly to Peel's foresight, promptness and determination. Even the *Freeman's Journal*, an O'Connellite newspaper that rarely found much good to say about any conservative, and Peel least of all, could pay him a retrospective tribute in 1847: 'No man died of famine during his administration, and it is a boast of which he might well be proud'.

The real test, however, was still to come. The failure of 1845, though widespread, had not been complete; and even in the affected areas the people, save the very poorest, had still some reserves, something left that they could pawn for food; and they were buoyed up by the hope that the next year's harvest would be plentiful. It was when the blight struck again, in August 1846, that despair became absolute. But by this time Peel was no longer prime minister. His break with the protectionists of his own party had compelled him to rely on the support of the whigs and radicals. With their help he carried the repeal of the corn laws, in June 1846; but almost at the same time he was defeated over an Irish coercion bill, which outbreaks of agrarian disturbance, not unnaturally provoked by the famine, had induced him to bring forward. In ordinary circumstances the protectionists would have welcomed such a measure; but they were so anxious for revenge on Peel that they readily joined forces with whigs and radicals, and even with repealers; and this 'blackguard combination', as Wellington called it, was strong enough to turn Peel out. In July, a whig ministry was formed under Lord John Russell; and it was this ministry that had to face the renewed crisis in Ireland.

(2)

When Russell took office there seemed to be some prospect of better times in Ireland; the weather in May and June had been warm, and the potatoes were flourishing. But the hopes thus raised were soon to be disappointed. 'On the 27th of last month', wrote Father Theobald Mathew early in August, 'I passed from Cork to Dublin, and this doomed plant bloomed in all the luxuriance of an abundant harvest. Returning on the 3rd instant, I beheld with sorrow one wide waste of putrefying vegetation. In many places the wretched people were seated on the fences of their decaying gardens, wringing their hands, and wailing bitterly the destruction that had left them foodless.' Similar tales of destruction and despair came from all over Ireland, for this time the failure was general. Weakened already by a season of unparalleled scarcity, and with all their resources gone, four million people faced the prospect of starvation.

This fresh disaster brought no immediate change in government policy. Trevelyan was still in charge of relief, and both the new prime minister and the new chancellor of the exchequer, Sir Charles Wood[1], shared his outlook. 'It must be thoroughly understood', wrote Russell in October 1846, 'that we cannot feed the people'. The government was prepared to promote public works, to help with the organisation of relief committees, and to make some financial contribution; but its basic thesis was that Irish poverty must be supported by Irish property. Such assistance as the government did give was, at first, made almost useless by the supposed necessity for conforming with the laws of political economy, as then understood. Thus, for example, no public money was to be spent on relief works that might be profitable to private individuals; and land reclamation and drainage, the improvements most likely to bring immediate benefit to the country, were thus excluded.[2] Again, relief committees were instructed not to sell food below the prices prevailing in their districts, lest the profits of normal traders should be endangered; and Peel's sensible, and partly successful, method of keeping down prices was abandoned.

The ineffective character of government action in Ireland, though resulting mainly from the economic principles on which it was based, had other causes also. Russell's parliamentary majority was precarious, depending as it did on the continued co-operation of inharmonious elements, originally brought together only by their antagonism to Peel; and even within the ministry there was divergence of view over Irish policy. In these circumstances, it might well seem that the safest course was to do as little as possible. And apart altogether from its political difficulties, the government suffered from an ignorance of Irish conditions so great that it might, by itself, almost justify the repealers' contention that Ireland could never be satisfactorily ruled from Westminster. What Russell, Wood and Trevelyan all alike failed to realise was that the economy of rural Ireland, especially in the areas most severely affected by the famine, was totally different from that of England. The peasant in these areas rarely handled money, and even more rarely used it for the purchase of food. He paid his rent by his labour; and he and his family lived on the potatoes that he grew himself. When the potatoes failed, he was helpless; and there was little use in paying him a money wage for his labour on relief works, without at the same time improvising a system of retail distribution that would enable him to turn his wage into food.

The notion that Irish poverty, in the crisis created by the famine, should be made a charge on Irish property displayed an equal ignorance of prevailing conditions. The government's readiness to criticise the landlords was understandable. Some land-

[1] Afterwards first Viscount Halifax.
[2] In 1847 this policy was modified; but the amounts of money actually advanced for reclamation and drainage were small.

lords simply disowned responsibility for the welfare of their tenants; some took advantage of the situation to clear their estates by wholesale evictions. But, whatever their attitude to the famine, they were not, as a body, able to bear the burden that the government wished to place upon them. Very many, perhaps a majority, habitually lived beyond their incomes; their estates were heavily mortgaged, and a large part of their rents was absorbed in the payment of interest. When, as naturally happened at this time, income from rents shrank, or disappeared altogether, they were faced with bankruptcy. To saddle them with the cost of famine relief might complete their ruin, but could bring little immediate benefit to their starving tenantry. What the landlords demanded (and on this point they were in unaccustomed harmony with the leaders of popular opinion) was that the cost of famine should be made a direct charge on the imperial exchequer: if Ireland was indeed an integral part of the United Kingdom, then the United Kingdom as a whole should be financially responsible for Ireland. It was a reasonable argument, but one that neither government nor house of commons would accept. The average British politican, however he might talk of the sanctity of the union, persisted in regarding Ireland as a distinct entity, and he looked with jealous caution on every proposal for the expenditure of 'the British taxpayers' money' on Irish objects.

If the people of Ireland had been left, during the bitter winter of 1846–7, to depend entirely on the cautious assistance of the government and the doubtful benevolence of their landlords, they would have fared even worse than they did. But a great deal was also done for them by voluntary effort. Societies, committees and individuals raised funds for the establishment of soup-kitchens, which for many months provided a large section of the population, especially in the west, with almost their only regular means of subsistence. A leading part in this work was taken by the Society of Friends—the Quakers—who set up central relief committees in London and Dublin in November 1846. These committees not only organised relief, but were careful to collect accurate information about the state of affairs: it was the reports sent in by Quaker agents in every part of the country that helped to enlighten British public opinion and the government about the true character of the situation in Ireland.

By January 1847 the cabinet at last began to realise that the measures so far taken were ineffective, and that a radical change of policy was needed; even Trevelyan was converted to the view that the provision of employment on relief works was no adequate answer to the problem, that the people must be fed, and that the cost of feeding them, now far beyond the range of voluntary effort, must be borne out of the public purse. The principle of local responsibility was not, however, to be abandoned; the provision and distribution of food was to be a charge on the rates; though the government would, where necessary, advance funds to start the new scheme, these advances were to be repaid, and running costs met, by the rate-payers. This new policy could only gradually be brought into operation, but by August over 3 000 000 people were being fed daily at the public expense. The burden was naturally heaviest in the poorer unions, many of which were now virtually bankrupt; for the collection of rates — difficult enough, especially in the west, even before the famine — had become almost impossible. By far the greatest part of the cost had therefore to be borne, in the first place, by the treasury; and though boards of guardians were made legally liable for the sums so advanced, most of this liability had, in the long run, to be cancelled.

In adapting the poor-law system to the situation created by the famine the government had had to abandon the 'workhouse test'; for though the workhouses were over-crowded, and though additional accommodation had been provided, they could not contain more than a tithe of those now dependent on public support. But the system of outdoor relief, reluctantly adopted, was intended as an emergency measure; its continuation throughout 1848, and until the late autumn of 1849, reflected the continuing pressure of famine. The potato did, indeed, escape the blight in 1847; but the area sown had been very small, and the crop, though particularly good, did little to relieve the situation. In one way, the absence of blight in 1847 had even an unfortunate effect. It revived popular faith in the potato, which was extensively sown in the following season, to the exclusion of almost anything else; so that when blight reappeared in the summer of 1848, and the crop was destroyed, conditions were as bad as they had been in 1846. By the end of 1849, however, though there had been a partial failure of the potato crop, the worst was over; and, for those who had survived, conditions gradually improved during the following decade.

(3)

In the gloomy picture of Irish society between 1845 and 1849 disease is an element no less important than hunger. The two had always been associated: typhus and relapsing fever[1] had long been endemic in Ireland; in any period of famine they spread with frightening rapidity; in the famine of the 1840s, more severe, more general and more prolonged than any that had preceded it, they ravaged the whole country. Both diseases are carried by the body-louse (though this fact was not recognised at the time), and in the crowded and filthy conditions generally

---

[1] Down to the nineteenth century the term 'fever' was commonly applied, without discrimination, to various diseases later differentiated by medical science. By the time of the famine the distinction between typhus and relapsing fever was well established; but even medical observers sometimes used the general term 'fever', or 'famine fever', without any more specific description.

prevailing in cabins, workhouses and hospitals a population whose resistance was already undermined by famine was fatally exposed to infection. Though these two were the most wide-spread and most deadly of the diseases that accompanied the famine, they were not the only ones; dysentery, for which Ireland had formerly been notorious, reappeared in epidemic form; scurvy, unknown while potatoes formed a staple article of diet, became common on their disappearance; famine dropsy resulted from extreme malnutrition, and occurred only among those who were actually starving.

The fever epidemics that marked these years began, as might be expected, among the famine-stricken poor, especially in the hard-hit western areas; but it was impossible to confine them within social or geographical boundaries. Typhus, in particular, attacked all sections of the population, and even proved more deadly among the middle and upper classes than among the peasantry. The swarms of beggars that patrolled the roads and flocked into the towns, driven from their homes by hunger or eviction, carried the seeds of fever wherever they went. It was, for example, an influx of such refugees that started an epidemic in Belfast, in September 1846, at a time when provisions in the town were still plentiful and cheap and when there was sufficient employment for the labouring classes.

Despite earlier experience of epidemics on a national scale (typhus in 1817–18, cholera in 1832), the medical services of the country were ill-prepared for the crisis resulting from the Great Famine. Each county possessed, or was supposed to possess, a county infirmary and a fever hospital; there was an infirmary attached to each workhouse; in most of the larger cities and towns there were hospitals founded by voluntary effort. Besides this, every part of the country had dispensaries, established and partly maintained by private subscription, and intended, in the first place, to provide free medical attention for the tenants and servants of subscribers. But this system, quite inadequate even in normal times, was completely overwhelmed during the famine. Hospitals were soon crowded to suffocation, for it was impossible to refuse the wretches who clamoured for admittance; and patients were packed into emergency accommodation in tents and 'fever sheds', outside the hospital walls, where they commonly lay on the bare ground, unable to obtain even a supply of water. Local officials and voluntary workers coped as best they could with these desperate conditions; and a specially-constituted Central Board of Health attempted, between 1846 and 1849, to improvise a national system of temporary fever hospitals. The attempt came too late to avert a major disaster, but it did something to mitigate the effect of the epidemics; and the high death-rate among hospital and dispensary doctors is evidence that, whatever the shortcomings of the medical services as a whole, individual medical practitioners did not shirk their duties.

It is impossible to calculate, with even approximate accuracy, the number of deaths from disease during the famine years. Hospital and workhouse records were often imperfectly kept; and even if they were complete, it would still be necessary to take into account the unknown thousands who perished in their own homes, or by the wayside, untended and almost unnoticed. It is equally impossible to calculate how many died from actual starvation; the number officially recorded, between 1846 and 1851, is 21 770; but it is certain that a very high proportion, and perhaps even a majority, of those who died from disease would not have contracted it in the first place, or would have survived it, had they been properly nourished. Taking into account all the available evidence, we may reasonably assume that between 1845 and 1850 not far short of 1 000 000 people died, either of disease or of hunger, as a result of the Great Famine.

The loss of population from the high mortality of the famine years was more than equalled by the loss through emigration. For thirty years before the famine emigration had been put forward, time and again, as the most obvious solution to the agrarian problem; but despite encouragement, and sometimes even pressure, from their landlords, Irish tenants had shown a strong reluctance to leave the country; and though a regular emigrant traffic had developed, the numbers were comparatively small: between 1841 and 1844 they averaged about 50 000 a year. The potato failure of 1845 hardly affected the situation, for there was a confident hope that the next season would be a good one; but the second failure, in 1846, produced a revolutionary change of attitude among the peasantry. Emigration, formerly a last desperate remedy, was now the first thing thought of; and there was an almost hysterical rush to leave the country, to escape, at all costs, from 'the doomed and starving island', and find safety elsewhere. In earlier years, emigrant sailings had been confined to spring and summer; and intending emigrants had made their preparations carefully. But, from the latter half of 1846 onwards, the panic-stricken crowds were clamorous to be off without delay; the traffic continued throughout the year; and thousands of helpless refugees put to sea with only the scantiest supply of provisions for the voyage, and without either means of subsistence or prospect of employment on their arrival. In 1846 they numbered 106 000, in the following year 215 000, and in 1851 the figure rose to a quarter of a million; though there was some decline after this, the volume of emigration remained very heavy during the rest of the century. Not all of this vast number could pay their own way: some were assisted by landlords anxious to clear their estates, some by the government; and, from 1849 onwards, remittances were coming in from earlier emigrants who had saved enough to enable them to pay the fares of relations they had left behind.

During the period 1846–51 about three-quarters of the emigrants went to the United States, the remainder to British North America[1], and the strain imposed on trans-Atlantic shipping by this sudden tide of emigration had disastrous results. Even if government, landlords and shipping companies had combined to render the transfer of population from Ireland to America as safe and as comfortable as they could, the emigrants would still have had to face considerable hardship; as it was, in the competitive conditions of a *laissez-faire* age, their sufferings exceed description. Hungry, verminous, fever-ridden, they were herded together on cargo ships hastily and imperfectly adapted to carry this human freight; and they were for the most part too ignorant and too apathetic even to attempt the most elementary precautions against infection. Inevitably, the rate of mortality was high — of emigrants sailing from Liverpool to Canada in 1847, one in fourteen died at sea, of those sailing from Cork, one in nine; and the bitter memory of the 'coffin ships' is firmly entrenched in the folk-tradition of the famine.[1]

The emigrants found that the end of the voyage was by no means the end of their troubles. Neither Canada nor the United States welcomed the mass influx of Irish, whose arrival was marked by fever epidemics which no quarantine regulations could prevent, whose innumerable sick and poor were an immediate burden on the public, and whose low standard of living threatened the security of the working class. But though generations were to pass before the Irish element in the North American population was to become fully assimilated, its cohesion and its rapidly growing numerical strength soon gave it, in the United States, a political importance that could not be ignored; and the rising influence of the Irish Americans had an important effect on the politics of Ireland.

The combined effect of disease and emigration was a sudden and catastrophic fall in population: in 1841 it had stood at 8 175 000 and the natural increase might have been expected to raise it to about 8 500 000 by 1851; in fact, the census of that year showed a population of 6 552 000. And the famine not only halted the process of growth, but completely reversed it: the decline continued steadily, and by the beginning of the twentieth century the population of Ireland was only about half what it had been on the eve of the famine.

(4)

Though the Great Famine was to have, in the long run, a revolutionary influence on Irish politics, the immediate effect of its onset was comparatively slight. During the winter of 1845–6

[1] There was some emigration to Australia during these years, but the total number (19,000) was insignificant.

[1] The philanthropist and educational reformer, Vere Foster, made the crossing as an ordinary emigrant in order to collect authoritative information about the condition and treatment of passengers.

political life continued to be dominated by the question of O'Connell's relations with the whigs, by the growing breach between Young Ireland and the Repeal Association, and by public controversy over the Queen's Colleges. In parliament, the repeal members showed less concern about famine relief than about Peel's coercion bill, to defeat which they were even prepared to jeopardise the repeal of the corn laws. The second failure of the potato crop, in 1846, brought a new sense of urgency; but even this hardly disturbed the existing political relationships. O'Connell, deeply moved by the sufferings he had witnessed, denounced Russell's relief measures as misguided and inadequate; but he did not break off relations with the ministry, to which he acted as a sort of unofficial adviser on Irish affairs. Both O'Connell and the Young Irelanders proclaimed the necessity for reuniting the repeal movement in face of a national calamity; but though their public utterances sounded magnanimous, in private negotiation neither side would give way to the other; the breach remained unhealed; and in January 1847 the Young Irelanders set up a rival organisation of their own, the Irish Confederation, under William Smith O'Brien, a protestant landlord, and one of the few members of the group who had a seat in parliament.

For a brief period it seemed just possible that this very rivalry between the two branches of the repeal movement would lead to a new and wider union. Both sides were anxious to enlist landlord support; for the idea of a national movement embracing all social classes, and drawing its leadership from the aristocracy and gentry, was still strong. And just at this time most Irish landlords were politically adrift. The dispute over the corn laws and the consequent break-up of the conservative party had temporarily weakened the link between Irish and British conservatives. And landlords in general, whatever their political allegiance, were uneasy about the government's policy towards the famine; they objected to the principle that Ireland should bear the financial responsibility for famine relief; and they demanded that public works undertaken in order to provide employment should be directed towards increasing the productivity of the land. On this latter point they were in substantial agreement with both groups of repealers; and members of both groups, eager for landlord cooperation, were very ready to join them. A meeting of peers, gentry and M.P.s of all parties was held in Dublin in January 1847, and called for a radical change in the government's policy towards Ireland. But if it seemed for a moment that a united Irish party was about to emerge, it soon became clear that the basis of union was too narrow; the conservatives were still conservative, and most repealers still clung to the idea of a whig alliance.

The political activity of this period, seen in retrospect, seems almost completely detached from reality. Irish society was in course of disintegration, and the grouping or regrouping of parties meant nothing to the thousands who were dying of starvation or fever. The maintenance of any kind of political organisation on a national scale had become impossible; and though a general election in the summer of 1847 resulted in the return of thirty-nine repealers, the repeal movement had by this time virtually ceased to count; the 'repeal rent' had dried up; and O'Connell himself was dead. In February 1847 he spoke for the last time in the house of commons, where his appeal for generosity towards Ireland was heard in respectful silence, though it had no effect on government policy; then, his mind occupied almost exclusively with thoughts of his approaching decease, he set off for Italy, resolved to spend his last hours in Rome; but death overtook him at Genoa, on 15 May.

O'Connell's great contribution to the development of modern Ireland was that he called into being, and organised for political action, the force of mass opinion; he taught the Roman Catholic majority to regard itself as the Irish nation; and all succeeding nationalist leaders, even when they have disagreed most strongly with his policy, have had to build on the foundations that he laid. It is easy to pick holes in his character. He loved power, and was not always scrupulous in his methods of gaining and keeping it; his policy seemed often to be guided by expediency rather than by principle; he was indefatigable in pushing the interests of his family and his friends, and he had an eighteenth-century tolerance of jobbery. But when all this has been said, he remains a man of transcendent genius, which he devoted to the service of his native land; no other single person has left such an unmistakable mark on the history of Ireland. And his influence was hardly less important on those who opposed than on those who followed him. The character of the revolutionary tradition, which he detested, and the political development of the protestant minority, which he attempted in vain to win over to repeal, were both affected profoundly, though in different ways, by the career and achievement of O'Connell.

O'Connell's death marked the end of a period in Irish politics; but the continuing activity of the Young Irelanders was to provide a postscript. During 1847 and the early months of 1848 they conducted intermittent negotiations with O'Connell's son, John —'the Young Liberator'—who now led what remained of the Repeal Association, with the idea of reuniting the two branches of the movement. But during the same period many of them were moving in a more revolutionary direction. John Mitchel, an Ulster protestant and the most militant member of the group, established in 1847 a new journal, significantly named the *United Irishman*. He had come under the influence of Fintan Lalor, a reformer who saw in the existing landlord system the root of Ireland's distress; and it was to the propagation of radical ideas on agrarian reform, and to preparation for an armed rising, that

Mitchel now devoted himself. At first, most of the Young Ireland leaders were alarmed at Mitchel's violent radicalism; but the easy success of the French revolution of February 1848 and the apparent strength of Chartism in Britain, combined with a growing conviction that no peaceful persuasion would ever induce the government to modify its policy in Ireland, made them think more favourably of rebellion. Mitchel himself was arrested on a charge of sedition, and condemned to transportation in May 1848; but almost immediately afterwards other Young Irelanders began preparations for a rising. They had neither the means nor the ability for the task; and they were too much out of touch with the temper of the country to realise that the famine had left the people in no mood for fighting. Their abortive attempt at rebellion, in the first week of August, ended in a brief skirmish with the police. Of the three principal leaders, one, John Blake Dillon, escaped to America; the others, Smith O'Brien and Thomas Francis Meagher, were taken prisoner. The government was too prudent to make martyrs; and though O'Brien was charged with high treason and condemned to death, both he and Meagher were, in fact, transported to Australia. But though the whole affair has about it an air of tragi-comedy, it is a not unimportant link in the tradition that stretches from the United Irishmen of 1798 to the Irish Volunteers of 1916.

While the Young Irelanders were planning impossible rebellions, a far more significant movement had made its appearance: in February 1847 a 'tenant-right association' had been formed in County Cork. The Irish tenant farmers had lost their enthusiasm for repeal, and they were not prepared to fight for a republic; but they were beginning to see the value of open and legal combination for the furtherance of their own social and economic interests.[1]

(5)

The decisive influence of the Great Famine on the economic and social life of Ireland arose directly from the sudden and continuing decline in the population: it was an effective, though terrible, solution to the problem of rural over-crowding. And yet, paradoxically, land became scarcer, not more plentiful; for though there were fewer people, there were also fewer holdings. Subdivision gave way to consolidation. In 1841 only one-fifth of the holdings had exceeded fifteen acres, by 1851 the proportion had risen to one half; but the total number of holdings had sunk from 690 000 to 570 000;[2] and in most parts of the country the process

---

[1] Below, pp. 345–5.

[2] The change between 1841 and 1851 appears from the following table:

Holdings	1841	1851
1–5 acres	310 436	88 083
5–15 acres	252 799	191 854
15–30 acres	79 342	141 311
above 30 acres	48 625	149 090

was a continuing one. The change was due partly to the land-lords, who were anxious to clear their estates, and who were helped by the relief legislation of 1847, which had denied public assistance to any person holding more than a quarter-acre of land, so that many small-holders were forced to give up their land in order to escape starvation. But the continuation of the process reflected a change in the character of Irish agriculture; from the 1850s onwards there was a fairly steady decline in tillage, with a corresponding concentration on cattle-raising, and in an agrarian economy based on cattle there was little place for the very small farm. Only along the western seaboard did condi-tions at all resembling those before the famine continue to exist; elsewhere, the multitude of tiny holdings was replaced by farms of economic size, and the ultimate establishment of a peasant proprietary in place of a landlord system was made possible.

The change in the distribution of land had important social consequence. In pre-famine Ireland, early marriage had been easy and common; subdivision of the family farm could provide each son with a potato-patch, and since he had no prospect of improving his position, he had no inducement to delay marriage. But in the altered conditions of the later nineteenth century, when it was considered essential to keep the farm intact, only one son could inherit, and he normally had to postpone marriage until his father died, or was ready to hand over the farm; for the other sons, and often for unmarried daughters also, emigration was the obvious resource. One consequence of this state of affairs is seen in a falling birth-rate; its general effect on the character of rural society, though it cannot be so easily assessed, was hardly less important.

Politically, as well as economically and socially, the famine had a profound influence on later developments. It left in the popular mind a feeling of resentment against the whole system of govern-ment in Ireland; and from this time onwards Irish nationalism takes on a new bitterness, particularly among the emigrants in America. O'Connell had paid tribute to the generosity and humanity shown by thousands of English people during the famine: 'If the exhibition of these qualities by invididuals', he wrote, 'could save Ireland in her present misery, we should be saved'. But, among Irishmen in general, gratitude for the aid afforded by English charity was overborne by a conviction that government policy had displayed a callous disregard for Irish suffering. Probably nothing did more to create and sustain this conviction than the government's refusal to impose an embargo on the export of food; and even at the height of the famine grain was being steadily exported from Ireland. Whether or not the imposition of an embargo would, by itself, have had much effect on the situation is open to some question. Those most in need of food had no money to buy it, however plentiful the supply — the very reason why Irish grain was being exported was that it had no market at home; and an embargo would have upset the whole economy. But no one could doubt that if a comparable crisis had arisen in England the government would have ensured adequate supplies of food, at whatever cost to the economy; or that an independent government in Ireland would have done the same. The Great Famine killed the repeal movement; but to succeeding generations of Irishmen it stood as a clear condemnation of the parliamentary union.

The British attitude to Ireland, as well as the Irish attitude to Britain, was affected by the famine. The widespread sympathy with the sufferings of the Irish poor was not unmingled with impatience, and sometimes with contempt. Even well-intentioned people so little understood the situation as to resent as folly or mere ingratitude the continuance of any Irish demand for self-government; and many would have accepted Trevelyan's verdict that 'the great evil' was not the famine itself but 'the selfish, perverse and turbulent character of the people'. The abortive insurrection of 1848 went far towards making this view general; and during the following winter, when the famine was as severe as it had been in 1846–7, there was a noticeable falling-off in voluntary contributions for relief. The anti-Irish feeling that had existed all through the famine in some quarters (it is reflected, for example, in the pages of *Punch*) now became stronger. Public opinion in Britain was coming to regard the Irish as irresponsible, ungrateful and treacherous, unfit to govern themselves, or even to enjoy the same constitutional rights as the rest of the United Kingdom.

When, in August 1849, the queen made her first visit to Ireland she was welcomed with enormous popular enthusiasm; but it would be a mistake to regard this enthusiasm as a true indication of Irish feelings towards Britain, and it certainly had no lasting effect on British feelings towards Ireland. As the two countries approached the end of a half-century of parliamentary union, they were, perhaps, more completely estranged from one another than they had ever been before.

from J.C. Beckett, The Making of Modern Ireland, 1603–1923 (Faber and Faber, London, 1966)

Skimming the chapter

Step 1 Look for *signposts*:

- the *title* of the chapter 'The Great Famine' will give you some idea of the content.
- the division into separate *sections* suggests that a number of separate but interrelated topics are covered.

Step 2 Read just the *first section* in full. Read quickly but with enough comprehension to be able to summarise it.

Step 3 Try now to *summarise* briefly the main points made in this section. Your summary will probably cover the following points:

1 The famine of 1845–9 was a major turning point in Irish history.

2 Failure of the potato crop was common but this time it was more severe, more widespread and longer lasting.

3 Government attitudes towards the famine and famine relief were complicated by domestic British political considerations.

4 Peel organised fairly successful relief measures but they were administered by officials acting on a *laissez-faire* philosophy.

5 The second year of the famine was more severe and came when there was also a change of government in England.

Step 4 Now read the following sentences:

The famine of 1845–9 is a major dividing-line in the history of modern Ireland.

From one point of view, there was nothing exceptional about the Great Famine save its extent and its intensity.

Though the dangers inherent in the Irish situation had long been recognised, no government had proved capable of working out any means of ameliorating it; and with the increase of population the margin of safety, always precarious, had grown narrower.

Difference of opinion about the seriousness of the potato famine did not arise solely from variation in the reports; there was a political reason also.

It is to Peel's credit that he did not allow personal or party interests to interfere with his plans for relief.

Though Peel took the initiative in these measures, their direction fell largely into the hands of Charles Trevelyan, assistant secretary to the treasury, and one of the new generation that was transforming the character of the British civil service.

The real test, however, was still to come.

In fact these sentences, which are the *opening sentences of each paragraph* in the section, provide you with a very similar

summary of the passage to that which you probably produced yourself after reading the section in full.

Step 5 What can you *conclude* from this exercise?

1 The opening sentences of paragraphs can often provide an
outline of the development of ideas in a passage.

2 Intensive reading of the same passage will provide more
detail and a fuller understanding of the argument.

Skimming the first sentences can provide you with sufficient grasp of the whole passage to decide whether:

1 it is relevant to your purpose, in which case you must
read it more thoroughly;

2 it has little relevance to your needs, in which case you
carry on skimming the next section until you do find a
relevant passage.

Step 6 Try this strategy once more. Read the *third section*
only and summarise briefly as you go. Compare your
summary with what follows — again a list of the first
sentences of the paragraphs in this section.

In the gloomy picture of Irish society between 1845 and 1849
disease is an element no less important than hunger.

The fever epidemics that marked these years began, as might be
expected, among the famine-stricken poor, especially in the
hard-hit western areas; but it was impossible to confine them
within social or geographical boundaries.

Despite earlier experience of epidemics on a national scale
(typhus in 1817–18, cholera in 1832), the medical services of the
country were ill-prepared for the crisis resulting from the Great
Famine.

It is impossible to calculate, with even approximate accuracy, the
number of deaths from disease during the famine years.

The loss of population from the high mortality of the famine
years was more than equalled by the loss through emigration.

During the period 1846–51 about three-quarters of the emigrants
went to the United States, the remainder to British North America,
and the strain imposed on trans-Atlantic shipping by this sudden
tide of emigration had disastrous results.

The emigrants found that the end of the voyage was by no
means the end of their troubles.

The combined effect of disease and emigration was a sudden and catastrophic fall in population: in 1841 it had stood at 8 175 000 and the natural increase might have been expected to raise it to about 8 500 000 by 1851; in fact, the census of that year showed a population of 6 552 000.

If you want more practice in this technique of skimming, try reading ONLY the first sentences of section 5 of the Beckett chapter (pp. 36–38) and turn to Appendix 2 to check your grasp of the passage.

Advantages of skimming

Skimming by paragraph units enables you to:

- decide quickly which materials you will read in detail and which can safely be skipped (time and selection problems);
- grasp quickly the focus and development of the writer's argument (comprehension problem).

Skimming is never a substitute for the close reading which some of your materials will require. But it does make it possible for you to read more flexibly and with more purpose.

You may find yourself feeling uneasy when you first start using skimming techniques. You may feel that you are 'cheating' in not reading every word that is on the page, especially if the book is by an authority on the subject. You may also be worried that you will miss some essential idea, and so 'cheat' yourself. However, these fears will be overcome once you recognise that skimming is a skill which you can adjust flexibly to your purposes. The greatest advantage of skimming is that it focuses your attention on the writer's own structuring of the material. This puts you in a position to make intelligent choices about what you will read, in what detail, and when.

Skimming for essay writing

When reading for an essay, you are reading with a definite purpose. You are not reading merely for the sake of interest or in the vague hope of coming across useful material. You are reading now in order to begin to find answers, however sketchy, to questions raised by the set topic.

At first these questions may be rather general. Our Pre-history topic

What light do you think can be shed on the early stages of human behaviour by the study of non-human primates?

would raise such initial questions as: what is known about the behaviour of early humans? what is known about the behaviour of primates? what seem to be links between these? and what is the evidence? Once you have begun to clarify your purpose in reading through specific questions, your skimming will become even more effective. And as you understand more about the subject, you will be able to redefine, develop or discard your initial questions. Your purpose in reading will become increasingly clear. At the same time your efficiency in skimming will increase.

If you want to check on the efficiency of skimming for an essay, look at the way you might use it for an essay based on the Beckett chapter.

1 Assume that you have been set the essay topic:

'The Great Famine was caused less by the failure of the potato than by human failure.' Discuss, in relation to events in Ireland in 1845–9 and to contemporary British politics.

2 Skim the whole Beckett extract in order to identify the material you think will be relevant to this topic.

3 Think over the following questions:

- How long, approximately, has this taken you?
- You would certainly want to go back and reread some paragraphs in more detail, but would you need to read the whole chapter in equal detail?
- Can you, even now, begin to develop an outline answer to the topic?
- Can you identify areas which you would need to cover in your essay which are not covered in this chapter?

If you want further practice in using skimming in relation to an essay topic, turn to Appendix 3.

Modifications of the skimming approach

Although you should find this method of skimming genuinely useful for much of your reading, it has some obvious limitations. It may be unsuitable for:

1 the study of *literary texts* or *primary historical sources* except at the most superficial level, since here the detail, the language and the cumulative effect of the writing are essential to your interpretation of the original.

2 the study of *Philosophy*, where the texts are often so densely argued that you need to unravel the reasoning sentence by sentence.

3 certain *styles of writing*, for example, some writers use the first sentence of a paragraph as a *bridge* from the idea developed in the previous paragraph to the idea which is to be developed next. Other writers, especially American authors of textbooks, use an *inductive* presentation in which the key sentence occurs more often at the end of the paragraph and is seen to develop from the preceding detail within the paragraph.

However, in such cases you should not abandon skimming altogether and merely revert to your previous habit of reading slowly and steadily from the first to the final sentence of the text. Even when faced with original texts or philosophical argument you can skim opening sentences and scan for key words or phrases to gain an initial understanding of the structure of the material. You may then want to go back and study the text in more detail.

When the problem seems to lie in the writer's style, rather than in the content of the writing, then you must vary your skimming strategy accordingly.

If you want to see how skimming can be modified to suit the style of a particular writer, turn to Appendix 4.

The structure of the paragraph

Let us return, finally, to the earlier definition of a paragraph in academic writing as an *idea unit*. The whole strategy of skimming is based on the recognition that a writer uses paragraphs as idea units to structure his or her argument and just as there is a structure in the development of an argument in an essay, so there is also a structure *within* a paragraph which is developing a single, central topic. This can be seen in the relationship between the individual sentences within the paragraph.

Look at the following paragraph from the Beckett extract and notice the logical ordering of the separate sentences:

The famine of 1845–9 is a major dividing-line in the history of modern Ireland. Politically, economically and socially, the period that followed it appears sharply distinct from the period that preceded it. In some ways this appearance is misleading: one effect of the famine was to concentrate in a few brief years changes that would otherwise have been spread over generations, and thus to disguise the real continuity between the two periods. But the very rapidity of these changes affected their character; and the immense burden of human suffering by which they were accompanied left an indelible mark on the popular memory. The historical importance of the Great Famine lies not only in the physical results that followed from it—the decline in population, the transfer of property, the changes in agriculture—but in the attitude to the government and to the ruling class that it engendered in the great majority of the people.

The diagram on the next page draws attention to the neat structure of this paragraph. Notice also the way in which the writer has 'signposted' the twists in the development of his argument: 'In some ways ... But ... not only ... but'. The lengthy sentences, broken into more meaningful and manageable units by colons, semicolons and dashes, also reflect the tight coherence of the separate points being woven into the argument. These are signs which alert you to the nature of this paragraph: it is presenting a controversial analysis of a particular historical event, not merely giving you information. It is leading you through a sequence of apparently conflicting views in such a way that you follow the writer's judgement and accept his assessment of the problem.

Had you been writing this passage yourself, you might have considered writing two separate paragraphs, possibly remembering rules from school days about 'one point only in each paragraph'. You might have written one paragraph on the points in common between the periods before and after the Famine, and another on the significant differences. However, if you think about it, such a division would have altered the whole intention of the writer: Beckett was using this paragraph as a unit to emphasise the inter-connections and complexity of contemporary attitudes to the Famine and of the more distanced historian's interpretation based on hindsight. He was focusing attention on the continuities, not the discontinuities.

You will notice that, although academic paragraphs are often long and complex (reflecting the complexities of the ideas being developed), they are very carefully structured

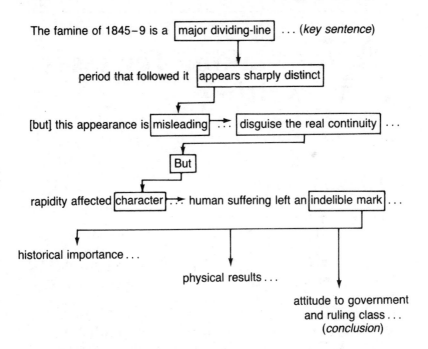

and linked. As we have seen, it is this systematic organisation of paragraphs which enables you to skim effectively.

Summary

In this chapter we have examined a variety of strategies for handling the reading which you must cover for an essay. We have suggested that skimming is the most effective skill you can develop for reading academic texts because it makes use of the paragraph as the basic unit underlying the structure of argument.

The main points to remember are:

1 Your lecture and tutorial notes and a reading list provide three useful starting points for your reading.

2 Careful analysis of the reading list will suggest sensible strategies for where and how to begin reading.

3 Skimming is the most effective initial technique for reading for academic purposes.

4 Efficient reading of academic texts depends on your ability to perceive the basic structure of argument which in turn is related to the use of the paragraph as an idea unit.

4

Note-taking for essay writing

Myth and reality

You will find, particularly if you are a first year student, that you are a natural target for dogmatic advice from lecturers, tutors, fellow-students and study skills books about note-taking methods. You will also find that there is little agreement among these well-intentioned advisers. Some will advocate the use of small cards to be kept in filing boxes and to be used according to a rigid system for identifying, recording and classifying each point noted. Others will insist that the use of complex systems of numbering and indentation is crucial. Others will express strong views about using different coloured inks, types of underlining, or methods of cross-referencing.

So which advice should you follow? Should you feel ashamed when your History lecturer, in your third year of study, exclaims at your inadequate note-taking skills because you do not use a card index? Or when your Geography tutor is appalled that you do not use both Roman and Arabic numerals in numbering your points? Or when fellow-students who have borrowed your notes complain that they cannot follow them? Or when your own notes bear no resemblance whatsoever to the neat model set out in a study skills book? In fact, note-taking is a peculiarly personal affair. You are recording information and ideas which *you* have decided suit your purpose. Therefore what you select and how you record it are matters of personal choice. You may pick up a few useful tips from looking at the methods other people use, but ultimately you must develop your own system. And, as you will see, your system must be sufficiently flexible to meet many differing purposes. These will vary with different disciplines, different sources and different tasks. They will also change according to the stage you have reached in your course and in your reading for the essay. (Here we are dealing solely with notes from printed sources. Lecture notes, though they may eventually be used as part of the material for your essay, are originally taken for a different purpose and therefore develop according to different criteria.)

Why do you take notes?

Think for a moment of the role note-taking plays in this long process of writing your essay. Why do you spend time recording material which is already available in printed form? There are both practical and intellectual points you might consider here.

1 Notes are an aid to memory. Obviously if you are reading for a long essay over a period of weeks, or for two or three essays simultaneously, then you must have some system of sorting and recalling information you will need when you finally come to plan and write the essay.

2 Your notes provide the raw material on which your mind must work in relation to your set essay topic. And you will need certain types of information, such as facts, figures and direct quotations, available quickly and accurately.

3 The process of note-taking forces you to:
- summarize ideas and arguments;
- select points relevant to your purposes;
- understand and interpret the original source;
- continually clarify and adjust your perception of your essay topic, in the light of your increasing understanding of the material and arguments presented by others.

So note-taking is an important stage in developing your understanding of your topic. Your notes will provide the basis for your thinking and the materials for your essay.

When do you take notes?

Again, the answer depends on your own purposes and the stage of reading you have reached:

- In your early stages of reading when you are skimming material of a general nature, you will probably not want to make any notes at all until *after* you have finished your skimming and have got a feel for the subject. Then you may find it useful to go back and make notes on the points or sections within the general survey which seem important to you.
- At a later stage of reading, when you can recognise more clearly the demands of your essay topic, you will probably switch to taking notes *during* reading, or at least at the end of each break in the passage.
- At times you may not want to take notes at all. You may prefer to photocopy a section from a book in order to underline key points or make marginal notes and cross-references to other materials. You will probably want to do this with essential materials or original texts which you must study in detail and refer to constantly. On the other hand, if you own the book you are reading, then your notes may be extremely brief: mere reminders of key points on specific pages, notes in the margins of the book itself, or even pieces of paper stuck between the pages.

What do you note, and how much?

The content and volume of your notes are governed by three considerations:

1 The **writer's intention** in the passage: The writer has selected and structured the material to meet specific intentions, but these are unlikely to be precisely the same as the focus of your essay topic. Therefore, while recognising the writer's own purpose, you must sift the information and ideas being presented according to your own interests. The same holds true for lectures and tutorials.

2 The **discipline** in which you are working: In disciplines in which you are working with original sources, for example History or Literature, you will have to include many direct quotations in your notes. As you will want to include some of these quotations in your essay, you must copy them with absolute accuracy. In other disciplines you will more often summarize passages in your own words.

3 **Your own purposes** in relation to your essay topic: If your purposes are clear, you can select and record relevant material in as much detail as you want. Some students insist that they prefer always to take detailed notes because 'it is all so interesting' or 'it may come in handy later' or 'the book is a standard text and so it is worthwhile spending time on it'. Well, maybe — but in practical terms you seldom have time to note everything you read in equal detail. You will find your notes more useful if they are shaped from the beginning by the demands of your essay topic.

How do you take notes?

So all that advice so confidently given about *how* to record notes is misdirected. Your notes will develop their own format, depending on your purposes and on the nature of the sources.

There are, however, three general principles which apply to all methods of compiling notes:

1 **Clear identification**: Your notes should be clearly headed with all the bibliographical details you may later need when you want to use these materials in your essay. In practice this means you must record the author, title, place of publication, publisher and edition, and date. And next to each key point or direct quotation you must note the exact page reference. (A fuller explanation of procedures for references is given in Chapter 7 and in Appendix 14.)

2 **Flexible system**: You should record your notes in such a way that it is easy to rearrange them for the purposes of your essay. Notes made on loose-leaf paper and cards have the advantage that they can be shuffled, combined and reorganised at the planning and writing stages of your essay.

3 **Room for comment**: Wide margins are useful. As you build up your materials you will find you want to add cross-references to other sources. You may also want to include your own comments or reactions to the text, or just indicate that a certain point may be crucial to your essay.

Summary

In this chapter we have dispelled a few of the common myths about fool-proof systems of note-taking. We have also recommended some basic criteria to help you develop your own note-taking methods.

The main points to remember are:

1 The guiding principle of your note-taking should be that the content, style, intensity and format of the notes suit the purpose for which you are taking them.

2 Your notes should be accurately identified, flexibly recorded and allow space for cross-referencing and comment.

5

Analysing and planning

Sooner or later you will arrive at the point when you need to switch from gathering material to planning how you will develop it into an essay. How will you decide when this critical point is reached? Isn't there time to read 'just one more book'? Or 'to wait for another week in case the topic is covered in a lecture'? You may feel very hesitant about actually committing your ideas to paper. Yet the more experienced you become as a student, the more clearly you will realise the danger of postponing the plunge into planning and writing.

In practice, you'll probably get started because you have to — because the deadline is dangerously close.

So what is the next step you must take?

Analysing your essay topic

You may find it useful to begin by going back to the essay topic not to look for clues about content but to analyse the ways in which you are being directed to use this material. What exactly is it that you are being asked to do with it all?

Look first for the key words which direct *how* the content is to be handled. For example, which are the key directional words in this Prehistory topic?

> Describe the hominid remains from the Koobi Fora sites. How do they compare with remains from other early African sites?

The first part of the topic seems to be straightforward. You are asked to *describe* prehistoric remains from a specific location. The terms in which you describe the remains and the characteristics you select for description (number? size? colour? shape? placement? etc.) would be those you were taught to use in the Prehistory course.

The second demand made in this topic is more complex. The directional word *compare* involves much more than mere description. It requires some form of *analysis*. For what purpose are you being asked to 'compare' two or more sets of hominid remains? Presumably to discover similarities and differences. And then to draw some general conclusions about what is significant in these points. Notice that the wording of the topic does not explicitly state that you must draw conclusions — but you will always be expected to do so. In other words, you are comparing the hominid remains in order to establish origins, causes and relationships. As soon as you begin to point to similarities and draw conclusions from them (for example, 'The remains at Koobi Fora and at X are so similar as to suggest that these hominids were derived from common ancestral stock . . .'), you are in the process of analysing your material.

The tasks of *describing* and *analysing* are common requirements in university essay topics. The task of describing may be identified by directional words such as 'explain', 'review', 'outline', 'enumerate', 'list', 'summarize', 'state'. Words which direct you to analyse your material include 'assess', 'compare', 'contrast', 'criticize', 'analyse', 'discuss'.

Look carefully now at these three essay topics. Can you recognise the point at which you are being asked to shift from describing your material to analysing it?

> The science of psychology is based on verifiable data. Experimentation is only one way such data is collected. Other methods include observation, surveys, tests, and case histories. Select one method and describe it at length, noting its advantages and disadvantages. (Psychology)

> List three methods of absolute dating and three of relative dating. For one of the absolute methods, describe how it is carried out, its application and its limitations. (Geography)

> What is a 'phoneme'? What is a 'morpheme'? Compare and contrast the status and function of the phoneme as the central unit of phonology, and the morpheme as the central unit of morphology. (Linguistics)

In addition to description and analysis, university essay topics commonly contain three other types of tasks:

- evaluation of controversy,
- definition or clarification,
- interpretation.

Evaluation of controversy

Look at the following topic from Political Science:

'Ministers provide a convenient facade for bureaucratic rule'. Do you agree?

This quotation contains a very strong value judgement. You can assume that it has been deliberately chosen or created for its provocative potential. This form of topic is very common: a strongly biased or controversial view of a complex issue is expressed and you are simply directed to 'discuss' it or asked 'Do you agree?' (The latter, of course, always includes the unexpressed 'or do you disagree?' and 'why?') This is a task of *evaluation.*

What are you being asked to 'evaluate' in this topic? The view that 'ministers provide a convenient facade'? 'Convenient' for whom? The ministers or the bureaucrats? Or both? 'Convenient' in what way? Ministers can always blame civil servants for bungles? Ministers are left by civil servants with responsibility for errors? What is a 'facade'? A front? Necessarily a *false* front? (Better check this in a dictionary . . .)

When dealing with a controversial statement, start by 'arguing' with it. Raise questions. Try to dig down to the implications and values underlying the wording of the topic. Get your mind moving on the issues. You will usually find you don't want to agree or disagree totally with a deliberately biased statement. In the Political Science question 'Do you agree'? not only includes 'or do you disagree?' and 'why?' but also '*to what extent* do you agree or disagree?' Totally? In part? With one, two, three reservations? With some minor objections?

Words and phrases which explicitly indicate the need for evaluation include 'to what extent', 'in what ways', 'how far', 'how valid', 'assess'. However, in some topics the demand for evaluation is only implicit. For example, if you were asked in Psychology to:

Review the factors (biological, environmental, and measurement) that are the primary sources of variation in IQ scores . . .

you would find, on the most superficial reading of the literature, that the biological source of variation in IQ scores is a highly controversial matter. Some authorities hold that it is the most significant factor of influence; others that it is the least. You will then realise that in order to 'review the factors' you must necessarily evaluate the conflicting views and evidence.

Look now at these topics and see if you can recognise what you are being asked to evaluate.

> 'Permitting unrestricted imports of goods produced by cheap labour is just like having migrants enter the country and take jobs away from citizens.' Assess this statement.   (Economics)

> Compare and contrast theories of learned versus innate aggression.   (Psychology)

> 'Donne's poetry is disagreeably self-centred.' Discuss any two of his poems, explaining how far you think this true of each (if not, why not) and how in each case this affects your judgement of the poem's merit.   (English)

> 'If we were to single out the crucial inventions which made the Industrial Revolution possible and ensured a continuous process of industrialisation and technical change, and hence sustained economic growth, it seems that the choice would fall on the steam engine and Cort's puddling process, which made a cheap and acceptable British malleable iron'. Explain why you agree or disagree with this statement.   (Economic History)

Definition or clarification

You will find that in most topics you have to clarify or define key terms or concepts before you can get down to the central task of the essay. However, in some essays the central task is one of definition and clarification. For example, this Philosophy topic:

> How do we know whether other people are happy? Can we know, beyond the possibility of illusion, whether we ourselves are happy?

Clearly these questions are directing you to define what we mean by saying 'people are happy', and what we mean by saying 'we know' something to be true. Equally clearly, simple dictionary definitions will not do. The whole task involves you in the process of gradually clarifying the nature of 'happiness' and the grounds on which 'knowing' rests. (If by 'happy' we mean X, then . . . but if we mean Y, then . . .) This process of definition is itself the answer to the questions you have been set.

Similarly, the following History topic:

Was there a 'revolution' in North America between c.1763 and 1800?

centres on the appropriateness of the term 'revolution' as a definition of certain events (revolution? evolution? rebellion? revolt? resistance?). This can be judged only in terms of your understanding of the events as presented in primary documents and other sources.

The following topics also involve tasks of definition. Which terms are you being asked to clarify in each question?

Is Scarlet and Black a story of success or failure? (European Literature and Society)

'Tools Makyth Man.' In the light of the present archaeological evidence what do you think can be said in support or criticism of this definition? (Prehistory)

Is the Presidency a 'democratic' institution? (American History)

Interpretation

Interpretation is closely related to translation. Literary criticism, for example, is largely an act of interpretation in which you explore the meaning and values created in a literary work in terms other than those of the work itself. Here is an exercise in practical criticism:

Write an account of Ted Hughes' poem 'Wind' which will consider, among other things, the central concern; the author's vocabulary; his use of imagery. Do you find his vocabulary and imagery appropriate, or artificial and overstrained, or original and stimulating? Are there any passages you would single out for praise or blame? For what reasons?

This exercise involves a certain amount of paraphrase (a restatement in your own words of the poem's meaning), critical comment upon the vocabulary and imagery of the poem, and judgement of the degree to which the poem is successful. All of these — paraphrase, critical comment, judgement — are part of the act of literary interpretation.

The task of interpretation may also be central to other disciplines. In History and Prehistory, for example, you may be asked to interpret primary documents or materials in relation to their period.

The following topics require, at some point, the task of interpretation:

> Analyse in some detail the opening paragraphs of <u>Bleak House</u>, concentrating upon the use of language and imagery.   (English)

> Make a critical examination of *one* article from any issue of the <u>Edinburgh Review</u> or the <u>Quarterly Review</u> between 1837–1850 which deals with a contemporaneous subject and show what it reveals about early-Victorian attitudes.   (History)

> Assess the contemporary significance of Radcliffe-Brown's 1925 paper on the Mother's Brother in South Africa.   (Anthropology)

Planning

It is useful to distinguish between 'planning' (a process) and 'plan' (an outline). 'Planning' takes place from the very beginning as you make choices among topics, as you read and select your material. A 'plan', on the other hand, is an outline of the way you propose to structure your ideas and information.

Plans can be drawn up at various stages of thinking about and writing your essay; planning is a continuous process. You will find that a tentative form of planning begins when you first analyse the topic. Even the way in which you ask yourself questions about the essay establishes some sort of order for collecting and recording information. As you read and take notes you become clearer about what parts the topic naturally falls into, or can reasonably be divided into. You will find yourself beginning to think about the way in which some of these parts relate to one another. Similarly, as you write you will be constantly shifting ideas and information about in your head, and on paper, to see why they fit best: deleting, expanding, writing, planning, re-writing.

Planning is in fact a creative process. It is the process by which you transform:

> the demands of the topic,
> the ideas of other writers, and
> your own thoughts

into your own original argument.

No one way . . .

There are as many styles of planning as there are students

writing essays. Here are three students describing the ways in which they work best:

David:
First I begin to read through my notes to get the ideas clear in my head. But this doesn't last long. I get bored going over the same old ground. So, even though I haven't sorted out my ideas, I start writing anyway. It's only after I've written a few paragraphs that I know clearly what I want to write. Sometimes it's more than that. Longer. It can take hours. But gradually the argument becomes clear as I write. When I've got it straight, I go back... Well, it depends. Sometimes I start again with it all clear, and sometimes I continue on to the end. Anyway I find I'm revising as I go because I know what I want to say.

Anna:
I write on coffee. I read over all my notes and then have a cup of coffee or take the dog for a walk. This lets the ideas bubble away at the back of my mind. Then I try and block out on a piece of paper the main points I want to make. I also put down the quotes and references I know for sure I want to use. I mean I put the ideas in the order I think I'll write them in. This is my outline I write from, you know, developing the ideas as I go but still coming back to the outline to check where I'm heading. Between coffee. I stop at each of the main sections and think again about where I'm going next.

Ben:
Well, I'm not so keen on working it out as you go along. I spend a lot of time thinking out the argument before I write a word. I make an outline. No, I make a series of outlines, building up the detail each time. And making the structure clearer. Then when I write, I try and get the first paragraph just right before I go on. Sometimes I work away at it for hours. Not just the same paragraph, but three or four different tries at it, till I think I've got it perfect. Or as good as I can. I do the same with each paragraph. I don't like thinking that when I get to the end I'll have to do the whole thing again. So I revise as I go. That's not always true, though. Sometimes I have to go back to the first paragraph because the argument changed a bit along the way. Mostly I try to keep the argument in line on the way through.

In fact all three strategies can be successful, but for different individuals. And it is misleading to suggest that one method is necessarily better than another. The one process that is necessary, and is achieved at different stages in all these approaches, is the *conscious ordering* of the material.

   You will notice also that in all three accounts the connection between planning and writing is extremely fluid; that even Ben, who has the most rigidly structured approach, is reshaping his material in the light of what emerges in his writing. In this sense planning and writing are truly inter-active, and creative, processes.

General planning strategies

Despite the wide variety of individual styles of planning, there are some strategies which seem generally useful. You may find the following system of working helpful. You can always adapt it as you go.

1 Analyse the essay topic. Check again how you are being directed to handle your material.

2 Read through all your notes. Do this both to remind yourself of material you may have read many weeks before and partially forgotten, and also to get an overview of the material which is now available for your use.

3 Begin to identify key points. There are various things you may wish to do at this stage. You may find it helpful to use the margins of your notes to make cross-references. You may want to underline or highlight points which you now see are important to your argument. Maybe you will write out the key points and quotations on a separate sheet of paper, or cut them out of your pages of notes. You could sort your notes into categories depending either on their common content or according to some gradually emerging order.

4 Think about a potential order for your material. Give yourself time to think about the significance of the materials you have collected. Think about the various ways in which they could be combined and ordered in relation to the topic. Think about the ways in which these materials seem 'naturally' to fall into a pattern. Think about the central aim of your argument and how your materials could be used to support and develop it.

5 Draw up a tentative plan. Block out on paper at least the main stages of your essay and a tentative conclusion. You may find it useful to include key names or points under each general stage. You may even want to pick out a particular quotation for your starting point. (But remember that this 'plan' is not a rigid guideline. It can be changed once you start writing.)

If you want to see a variety of plans for a common essay topic, turn to Appendix 5.

Finally, you may be disappointed to discover that there is no single foolproof method of planning your essay. Don't be. It means that you can forget the nagging worry that there is some 'skill' in this whole business of thinking and writing which, if only you can obtain it, will set you up for academic life. In fact most essay topics do have an inherent structure which emerges, almost spontaneously, as you work through the materials. Each time you write an essay you are faced with the same difficulty of discerning this structure and shaping it to your purposes.

Summary

In this chapter we have looked at the related stages of analysing your essay topic in order to identify what you are directed to do with your material, and of working towards a tentative plan for your essay. We have stressed that planning is a process that takes place continuously throughout the preparation for and drafting of an essay. And that there is no one style of developing a plan which is 'the best'.

The important points to remember are:

1 You need to analyse your topic carefully.

2 Most essays involve both description and analysis.

3 Other common tasks in essays are evaluation of controversy, definition and clarification, and interpretation.

4 Planning is a process by which your ideas, your materials and the demands of the set topic are transformed into an original piece of writing.

5 At some stage in the production of your essay you must develop a conscious plan, but how and when you do this depends on your individual style of working.

6 There are some steps which are useful in developing an essay plan, including close reference to the topic, reading over all your notes, and developing a tentative sequence of content.

6

Drafting and redrafting

All writing involves hard labour: what T.S. Eliot calls the 'intolerable wrestle with words and meanings'.

By the end of secondary school you had probably developed a good system for working on essays. But university essay writing imposes new demands. As we have seen, the topics are more complex, and you are required to do a lot of independent reading and research. In addition, the essays are usually much longer than those you wrote at school, which raises new problems of structuring your material. And there are conventions of style and scholarship (use of bibliographies, references, etc.) which may be unfamiliar. You will need to adjust your system of writing to meet these demands.

For a start, you can no longer get by with only one writing (draft) of an essay. You'll need to write at least two drafts because the first and second drafts are written for different purposes. In the first draft you are writing primarily for *yourself*: writing through the material in order to impose an order on it and to see, at the end of it all, exactly what you think. In the second, and possibly subsequent drafts, you are much more aware of your *reader* — your tutor or lecturer. At this stage you are constantly adjusting the style, tone, presentation and other features of the essay to meet his or her expectations.

All writing involves a writer, a content and a reader. What distinguishes one type of writing from another is the context in which it takes place. The special characteristics of essay writing in an academic context are shown in the diagram on page 61.

Context: You are now writing in a discipline within a university. Therefore you are immediately constrained in terms of your purpose, the content you may use, your voice, style and language. For example, the voice you adopt to present your argument must be a combination of your own personal voice and the specialist voice of the discipline — the voice of the sociologist, the philosopher or the literary critic.

Characteristics of academic essay writing

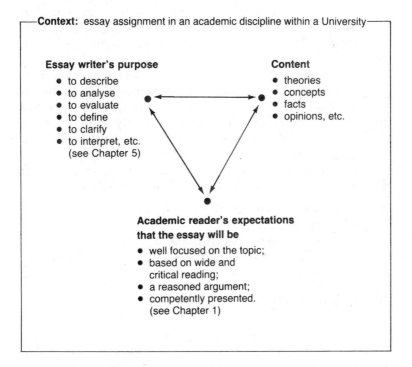

Context: essay assignment in an academic discipline within a University

Essay writer's purpose
- to describe
- to analyse
- to evaluate
- to define
- to clarify
- to interpret, etc.
  (see Chapter 5)

Content
- theories
- concepts
- facts
- opinions, etc.

Academic reader's expectations that the essay will be
- well focused on the topic;
- based on wide and critical reading;
- a reasoned argument;
- competently presented.
  (see Chapter 1)

Writer's purpose: As a university student your primary purpose in writing is to present a reasoned argument based on evidence. You might also have a more specific purpose in mind, such as justifying your view that one of Donne's poems is better than another, or that one pricing scheme for medical services is better than others. Also you'll be aiming to get a high mark. But your overriding purpose — presenting a reasoned argument — is governed by the context in which you are writing and your reader's expectations.

Reader's expectations: These have been set out in detail in Chapter 1. There is necessarily a tension between your purposes as a writer and your reader's expectations. You are trying to draw your reader in the direction of your conclusion. The reader, though open to conviction, will be constantly checking the track of your argument for such features as consistency, logic, use of evidence and clarity.

Content: Just as your purpose and your reader's expectations are shaped by context, so too is your content. This content is not the fruit of your naked wit or imagination but the material you have already collected in your reading. Now you must manipulate it and present it in a way that will achieve your purpose.

It is the way in which you shape this material to support your own argument that gives your essay its stamp of 'originality'. You are not expected to discover original material in your reading and research. But you are expected to construct your argument out of the material you do find. In so far as it is your own argument, it is original.

So the quality of your essay will be judged by the extent to which you have satisfactorily balanced these four factors.

- the **context** in which you are writing,
- your **purpose** in writing,
- your **reader's expectations**, and
- your selection, arrangement and presentation of **content**.

The first draft

The first draft involves writing to understand what you think. It is written largely for yourself. This does not mean that you may totally ignore your reader. Rather it means that your primary focus is *inwards* at this stage. You are conscious, above all, of a voice in your own head which is 'thinking aloud': sorting through the material, selecting and rejecting, planning, ordering and rearranging; trying out alternatives for the next words; looking backwards and forwards over the sentence you are presently constructing, seeing if it sounds right, if it says what you are trying to say; wondering how you'll get from the idea you're writing now to the next idea you vaguely know is looming up.

Because you are focused inwards in your first draft, attending to this internal voice which is making sense of your material and fashioning it into an argument, you cannot attend at the same time to the demands of your reader. At this stage you are still sorting out your own ideas. You are not yet ready for anyone else's criticism. In redrafting, you will need to give attention to the most appropriate ways of presenting your argument to your reader. But for the moment concentrate on 'talking' your way, however tentatively, through the whole argument.

In summary, therefore, it is a useful strategy to regard the first draft of your essay as a private matter. This draft is not your last word on the subject. It is not even written for criticism by anyone but yourself. It represents one stage in the development of your ideas. It can, and certainly will, be changed, rearranged and improved. But it is a start.

Stumbling blocks

1 Inability to get started. You'll probably hear your friends complain, 'Starting is the hardest part. If only I can get that right, I can go on.' Some writers scratch away at the first paragraph for hours, searching for the perfect opening. But you shouldn't be aiming at perfection in your first draft of an essay.

Why not try writing the introductory paragraph very quickly, so that you can get on to the real content of your essay before you give up in frustration? At this stage it is important to get your ideas and words flowing. Later you will have to come back and rewrite your introduction anyway, in the light of your conclusion. That will be the time to polish it to your heart's content.

2 Getting stuck part-way through. There will be times when you are stuck, trying to find the right word or a neat way of linking two points. That's inevitable. But there may also be times when you feel totally stuck. You do not know what should come next. This can happen when you have come to the end of one section of your essay and are looking for some way of bridging to the next. Maybe you just need a break. If this doesn't work, try talking the problem over with someone — perhaps a tutor or fellow student. It does not really matter whether the listener is familiar with the subject matter of your essay so long as he or she can ask intelligent questions. Often in the very act of discussing the problem, the solution occurs to you.

If none of this works, go and see your lecturer, who may be able to point to some important concept which you have missed altogether or partially misunderstood. Most academics are ready to help if they can see you have really tried to solve the problem for yourself.

3 Finding part-way through that your reading and note-taking have been inadequate. There may be two aspects to this problem: the first resulting from a fundamental gap in your reading; the second from poor planning.

If you become aware that there is a genuine gap in your reading, then you're stuck. You have no real alternative but to go back and do the reading. If, however, the missing material is not essential at this stage (for example, a quotation which you can only vaguely remember but which you know supports your point), then it is safe to continue with your writing and merely note in the margin that something must be looked up and inserted later.

If you find that you are constantly referring back to your notes as you write and — more than that — that you are constantly shuffling through pieces of paper looking for ideas or quotes you half-remember, bits of information you 'know you have somewhere', then your planning has let you down. You'll probably have to take time off and organise your notes and materials more effectively.

4 Your initial argument goes sour or you lose the track. These are two different but related problems. If you suddenly realise that your argument is drying up or that it is going in the wrong direction and your evidence no longer supports it, what can you do? You can just struggle on, hoping your reader will not notice the weakness. Or resign yourself to doing more work. This does not mean that your work so far has been totally wasted. What you have to do is rethink your argument on the basis of these same materials and then replan and rewrite in line with your improved understanding.

The second problem — losing the track of argument — is easier to solve. You must go back to a point in the essay where you are confident about your argument. Then ask yourself 'What should come next?' You can usually pick up quite quickly the point at which you wandered into the side-track. You may, in the course of writing, have been diverted by an idea which is only on the fringe of your essay topic. Or you may have used a relevant example but then chosen an irrelevant point from it to develop as your next step. Whatever the cause of the problem, you must go back until you are on course again.

If none of these strategies works, then again you are in need of outside help.

5 Running out of stamina. Thinking and writing are exhausting. The strategy of taking frequent breaks seems sensible and tempting. On the other hand, you often need to push on and on, uninterrupted, in order to keep up the momentum of your argument. Too many short breaks, or even one long break in the course of the first writing, may disrupt your thinking.

There seems no easy answer to this problem. Writers develop all sorts of individual strategies for coping with it. Some allow themselves frequent breaks but only after they've sketched out the beginning of the next section. Others simply struggle on to the point of exhaustion. Others depend heavily on cigarettes, coffee or chocolate. Others promise themselves rewards once they have finished. You'll have to devise your own strategy for keeping going. Continuity is important in the first writing.

Redrafting

The first draft is complete. You are probably not very happy with it, but it is a relief to have something down on paper. At this stage you need, above all, to distance yourself from your writing. If you can, put the essay away for one or two days. Your mind will continue to turn the ideas over, but more coolly. When you do come back to the essay, you will find it easier to look at it critically.

There is a sound reason for this need to become detached from your argument and material. Until now you have been writing for *yourself*, satisfying yourself about what you think. Now you must shift your focus and begin to consider how to satisfy someone else, the *external* reader and critic.

Will my argument satisfy the reader? Is it relevant? Is it logical? Is it clear? Does it flow? Is it well expressed? Does it meet the 'lecturers' expectations' set out in Chapter 1? At this stage you should still only be concerned with questions related to the quality of your thinking and style. The final details of presentation should be left to the later stage of editing (see Chapter 7).

So how can you set about revising your first draft effectively? You could start by asking yourself these two questions about what you've written:

1 Is it *intellectually* convincing?

2 Does it *sound* convincing?

The following checklist should help you to identify those parts of your draft which need redrafting. The lefthand column sets out the questions you need to ask about your argument and style, and the righthand column suggests some practical strategies for finding solutions to these questions. In some cases the strategies are self-explanatory. In others a more detailed explanation is given in the pages which follow the checklist.

Checklist for redrafting

Question 1 Is it *intellectually* convincing?	Practical strategies for finding solutions
Scope and focus:	
(a) Is your draft too short or too long?	Expand or prune (see p. 67–8)
(b) Have you answered the question?	Skim quickly through your notes. Read through any outline you have made. Read the draft again, making notes in the margin where changes seem necessary. (You will need to take all of these steps to answer questions (b) and (c) satisfactorily.)
(i) Have you answered the *whole* question?	
(ii) Have you answered questions other than the one asked?	
(c) Have you covered all of the important areas noted in your reading?	

Logic and structure:

(d) Is there a clear thread of argument running through your essay?	Construct a summary of your argument based on the paragraphs (see p. 68–9)
(i) Do the separate parts relate logically one to another?	Ask another reader for a second opinion.
(ii) Is there a satisfactory balance in the development of your argument?	
(e) Does your essay have an effective introduction and conclusion?	Read the first and last paragraphs and check that they reflect the key concerns of the topic (see pp. 69–75).

Question 2 Does it *sound* convincing?	**Practical strategies for finding solutions**
(a) Is your phrasing precise and accurate?	After your *second* draft, read quickly back over one or two pages from your sources (to reacquaint yourself with the voice of the disciplinary specialist). Then read your own essay *aloud*. Ask another reader for a second opinion.
(b) Are the voice and style you adopt:	
(i) appropriate?	
(ii) consistent?	

Practical strategies

Question 1 Is it *intellectually* convincing?

1(a) Is your draft too short or too long?

Variations of approximately ten per cent above and below the prescribed number of words are generally acceptable. In setting the word limit on an essay, the lecturer is giving an indication of the extent of detail required. If, therefore, you are well over the number of words set, this may be a warning that irrelevant material has crept into your essay or that your style is verbose. (Not always, of course; maybe you have done a great deal more reading than the lecturer expects of average students.) If you are well below the number of words, this may be a signal that you have left out part of the question or an important area of material, or that your style is too clipped.

So, if you find you need to *expand* the number of words:

- See if there is an area of content which you have left out or one which can be expanded.
- See if the general points you are arguing need further evidence or more detailed examples.
- See if your essay needs more detailed background information on which to base your analysis. You may be assuming that your reader's knowledge of your material is greater than in fact it is.
- See if you need to make your argument clearer for your reader by making the links in your reasoning more explicit.

If you find you need to *reduce* the number of words:

- Look for irrelevancies and repetitions, and prune vigorously.
- Look for lists of evidence and examples which could be covered by a brief generalization.
- Look for explanation, background and assumptions which may be cut out or covered by a reference.

1(d) Is there a clear thread of argument running through your essay?

     (i) Do the separate parts relate logically to one another?

     (ii) Is there a satisfactory balance in the development of your argument?

Read through your draft, asking yourself at the end of each paragraph: 'What is the main point in this paragraph?' Then write a one sentence *summary* of each of your paragraphs. This summary is valuable: it tells you what you *have* said, which may be surprisingly different from what you *intended to say*. It will soon show you:

- whether your argument is consistent;
- whether the connection between one point and another is clear;
- whether your ideas are in the right order;
- whether your ideas are organised into paragraph units;

- whether one section is unnecessarily long (maybe the opening section?);
- whether the discussion of theory and concepts is adequately balanced by the use of examples;
- whether one aspect is treated in much greater detail than another (is this justifiable?).

In some of your essays you may gratefully recognize that little renovation is necessary because the essay, as it stands, is reasonably well-organized and clear. Other essays may require much greater reorganization because your thoughts and your material only gradually took shape as you were in the process of writing. Most commonly you will find that some sections of your essay are almost totally acceptable and need only minor revisions, and other sections need much more drastic rewriting.

There may be times when you feel so unsure of your own judgement about the quality of your draft that you want to get a *second opinion*. This is a sensible strategy. Don't be hesitant about using it. Some students feel reluctant to ask other people to read a draft of their essay, maybe because they feel ashamed of it, or don't want to waste other people's time, or feel it is somehow 'cheating'. But you are not asking anyone to write the essay for you. You are merely asking for constructive criticism. You are doing what all academics do with their own writing. It is one of the best ways of testing out and clarifying ideas.

Appendix 6 contains an example of one student's attempts to reorganize a first draft.

1(e) Does your essay have an effective introduction and conclusion?

Why do essay writers find the first and last paragraphs of an essay so difficult? 'If only I could get my introduction straight, then I could go on.' 'My conclusion just seems to repeat the opening.' 'What are you supposed to do in a conclusion anyway?' 'What do they mean "round off" your essay?' 'How can I be original and dramatic in the opening?'

The introduction and conclusion are key points in your essay; maybe that is why you feel so reluctant about writing them. First and last impressions do matter. So what should these paragraphs include?

Introduction

Let's begin by looking at what some students actually do in writing a first paragraph. Compare these two openings which appear to have a similar general purpose; that is, to establish the writer's attitude towards the sources being used in the essay.

Example 1, Anthropology topic:
Do you regard the distinction between religion and magic as valid? Discuss with reference to two examples.

Opening: The distinction between magic and religion is one that has been debated amongst anthropologists for many years. Most anthropologists have been prepared to accept Frazer's (1976:220) proposals as an explanation of the difference. In more recent times it seems that the approach is to study magic and religion as a unity. The statement that both magic and religion should be treated together as 'magico-religion' seems to encapsulate the present approach (Titiev, 1979:334). The problem of validating the distinction between magic and religion presents many difficulties.

Example 2, Prehistory topic:
Discuss the ways in which studies of a contemporary hunter-gatherer group may help us to understand the archaeological record. Apply to a contemporary hunter-gatherer group.

Opening: If observations of living groups are to be of use in helping us to reconstruct prehistoric life-ways, great care must be taken when interpreting the ethnographic evidence. It is a risky business to assume that because certain socio-cultural patterns are apparent in modern groups, that these must have parallels in their prehistoric equivalents.

The differences are striking. Example 2 is a clear, though carefully qualified, statement that there are 'risks' in drawing inferences about Prehistory from contemporary human societies. It seems that the writer intends to look especially at 'socio-cultural patterns', and you would be justified in expecting her to make explicit, with examples, just what those risks are. In other words, you have been given some understanding of the writer's point of view and you have some indication of the area in which she intends to apply it. Example 1, by contrast, fails to make a clear and comprehensive statement about the topic. The writer states that there is a division of opinion or judgement amongst the sources he has consulted: on one side Frazer and others who regard the distinction as valid, on the other Titiev who does not. Yet the writer fails to tell us clearly whether he himself believes such a distinction is valid — let alone suggest what that distinction might be. The impression given is less one of caution (compare Example 2) than of confusion. After reading this introduction we are still unsure what the writer is going to argue in his essay.

Two more examples of introductions, this time both for the same topic, are discussed in Appendix 7.

Look now at an opening paragraph from an essay in a Greek civilization course. The lecturer's comment on this was: 'A superb introduction: clear, intelligent, and perceptive'.

> **Topic:** Fifth century Athens is usually considered to have been the birthplace of 'democracy', but the term 'democracy' has come to have a variety of connotations. Discuss the nature of Athenian democracy of the 5th century B.C.: its ideals and its actual workings. (Useful comparisons or contrasts with modern democracy will be welcomed but not obligatory. Beware of unsupported generalisations.)
>
> **Example 3, Opening para:**
> The Athenian constitution of the fifth century was remarkable for the democratic principles it embodied — hitherto unheard of. The ideals of any society are difficult to evaluate without over-simplification; however, four main principles can be discerned in fifth century Athens: sovereignty of the citizens, equality, liberty, and justice for the citizens. A greater insight into the nature of the democracy can be achieved by examination of its more important institutions: the Assembly, electoral eligibility, electoral method, duration of office, ostracism and the liturgies. This century some have disputed the validity of Athenian democracy, one reason being the exclusion of women, metics, and slaves from participating in government. However, the difference between fifth century Athenian government and a Western twentieth century democracy lies not essentially in the theory behind the constitution but in the definition of a citizen.

Here you have been given an impression of the probable development of the whole essay: a discussion of the nature of Athenian democracy, looking at its principles and its major institutions; then an examination of modern criticisms of the political system; and, finally, some comparison between Athenian democracy and modern theories of democracy. Notice also how skilfully the writer has suggested the order in which she will develop her ideas, without explicitly saying 'First', 'Second', 'Third', 'Next', 'Finally', etc.

Your reaction to the Athenian democracy essay may have been: 'I wonder if I could write an opening as clear as that'. In fact you could — but only with practice, and only if you understand what the special tasks of the introductory paragraph are. From the discussion of actual examples here and in Appendix 7, you can recognize two of these tasks:

1 Your first paragraph should focus your reader's attention on the central themes of your essay and express a clear point of view.

2 It should give the reader some understanding of the order in which you are going to develop your ideas.

These are essential tasks. You may sometimes also want to do other things, such as define a central term or concept, or use a key quotation as a starting point. It is usually only when you have completed your first draft that you can see clearly what needs to go into your first paragraph. Even then, it may take you two or three revisions to create an opening that really satisfies you.

For an example of the stages of redrafting one student went through in writing her introductory paragraph, see Appendix 8.

Conclusion

Your essay cannot merely come to a stop. You must draw it to a conclusion. In the body of the essay you have been developing your argument in detail. The concluding paragraph must pull together all of those details into a general statement which sums up your argument. It should refer your reader back to the topic. This gives your essay a sense of unity.

Because it is your final word on the topic, the last paragraph can make a great impact on the reader. This potential impact will probably be lost if:

1 The final paragraph merely presents the development of a minor point in your argument — for example, this conclusion to a Sociology essay comparing the structures of group and sub-group norms:

Example 4
Having shown the importance of the external system and interaction upon sub-group development, I now finish with another allusion to the negative effect of an absence of interaction. The

researchers were able to perceive that the group studied, the isolated group, were being treated with increasing antagonism by the rest of the department and, true to form, they perceived themselves as an isolated unit within which they must seek identification.

2 The paragraph ends with a lengthy quotation, which may mean that you have been working towards someone else's conclusion — for example, this conclusion to an Anthropology essay on distinctions between tribal, peasant and modern societies:

Example 5
Other traditional structures persist, as noted by C. Nakani (1967, p. 172):
'Many particular aspects...are disappearing from rural life today, owing to expansion of industrialisation. However, the distinctive characteristics of Japanese social structure...in their rural milieu are, in my view, persisting in various modern communities such as factories, business firms, schools, intellectual groups, political parties, etc...'

3 The paragraph is so cryptic as to be 'clever' without depth — for example, this concluding two sentence paragraph of an Anthropology essay on the nature of 'exchange' in traditional society:

Example 6
The basis of exchange is many things and no single thing. The best we can say is that the basis of exchange is a dialogue acted on a cultural stage.

While your conclusion is shaped by the need to reacquaint your reader with the major themes of the essay and your overall point of view, the actual strategies for concluding may be as varied as those introductory strategies we examined earlier. Here, for example, is a conclusion which seems to work well. The writer not only takes us back to the central terms of the topic but also makes clear that his exploration of the topic has led him to a redefinition of it. The central question of slavery, he suggests, is never one of relative degrees of humanity but of relative degrees of economic advantage to the slavers.

Example 7
Topic: What were the unique features of slavery in the British North American colonies, as contrasted with slavery in the French, Spanish, and Portuguese colonies? Under which colonial slave system would it have been preferable to be a slave?

So the question of which was the preferable slave system is really unanswerable. It would depend on what was of prime importance to the individual, the greater chance of legally acquiring his freedom or the stronger possibility of survival. In practical terms the overall deciding factor in the actual treatment of slaves was the economic one. In French, Spanish and Portuguese colonies it was cheaper to replenish stocks of slaves by purchasing rather than breeding them. In North America it was generally found a better policy to look after the slaves one had and to foster their breeding. In the long term 'humane' slave codes provide little protection against the greed of the master.

Another strategy is simply to refer to a key word or phrase in your introduction. Or you can relate the structure of your conclusion to the structure of your opening. Here is an example of this technique from a student's History essay:

Example 8
Topic: What can be learned about life in England in the late eighteenth century from Mary Wollstonecraft's *The Wrongs of Woman: or, Maria*?

Opening: Upon her death in 1797 from complications arising out of childbirth, Mary Wollstonecraft had completed only fourteen chapters, or Part I, and sections of Parts II and III of her second novel *The Wrongs of Woman: or, Maria*. This fictionalised version of ideas on the position of women in society gives us a valuable insight into some of the social conditions of the age. We are made aware of the oppressed position of women in relation to property rights, of their exclusion from formal education, their boredom and dependency, their entrapment within marriage, as well as learning something of the horror of social institutions such as hospitals and mental asylums. Yet, how complete and faithful a record has Mary Wollstonecraft presented? Are there not elements of sensationalism and melodrama — partly deriving from the literary tradition within which she was writing — which give us a biased and unrepresentative picture of her society? Is her picture selective in terms of class, and if the society in which she lived was so repressive of women, how is it that she was able to write and publish such a book?

Conclusion: *The Wrongs of Woman*, therefore, is an attempt explicitly to document the social, economic and legal position of women of all classes in English society during the latter part of the eighteenth century. It successfully establishes the oppression of at least some women of the time; their 'dependence next to menial'; their boredom, lack of education and resultant flights into romanticism, and, above all, the discriminatory power of laws relating to property. However, there are two clear limitations on the novel's usefulness as an instrument for revealing the age in which it is set. First, it is incomplete, both in its intended design and in the breadth of social life it describes. Working-class women we have in plenty, but where are women of the highest classes who might be the most obvious victims of legal discrimination? Second, the novel's literary failures—the characters are stilted and the events held together by the barest of threads—mean that we get very little detailed understanding of the people, their attitudes and reactions to social conditions. The novel is a disguised tract, and therefore decidedly exaggerated. If things were as bad for women as Mary Wollstonecraft suggests, this book would never have seen the light of day.

The opening paragraph begins, appropriately, with the writer placing her subject in an historical context. She then sketches the basis on which an argument for the novel's usefulness as a source of history might be constructed. Finally, (the conjunction 'yet' signals a change in direction) the writer raises a number of questions, suggesting the need for caution in evaluating the accuracy and completeness of the work as an historical record.

The concluding paragraph closely reflects the structure of the introduction, though there are subtle differences in the strength of the views advanced in each. The first part of the paragraph affirms the book's usefulness in illuminating the life of certain contemporary women. That part of the case, at least, has been established. The second half of the paragraph firmly answers the questions raised in the second half of the introduction. The writer concludes that inherent weaknesses in the design and style of the book result in selectivity and bias. By creating a conclusion which reflects so closely the structure and central themes of her introduction, this writer has given the whole essay a sense of unity and completeness.

Question 2 Does it *sound* convincing?

2(b) Are the voice and style you adopt
    (i) appropriate, and
    (ii) consistent?

'Style' may be used to describe a particular type of writing distinguished by its function or context (legal style), or to refer to some general features of writing (clarity is 'good style').

When you get an essay back covered with such comments as 'Poor expression', 'Awful!', 'Cliché', 'Jargon', 'A bit pompous?', your lecturer has been irritated by your style. How can you improve it? What is 'academic style' anyway?

At the beginning of this chapter there was a diagram showing the relationship between writer's purpose, reader's expectation, content, and the context of writing. The distinctive features of academic style are closely related to these four factors. For example, in an academic context language is used to express analytical and abstract thinking. For this reason you will find lengthier and more complex paragraphs and sentences in an academic paper than in, say, an army instruction manual. The purpose of the manual is to issue instructions; lengthy complex sentences are not the best means of doing this.

Let us tackle this matter of distinctive styles in a more practical way. Read this paragraph from an academic journal:

Extract 1
What are the anatomical bases for the human communication system? Asymmetry of the brain has been linked with language and speech and was once considered a distinguishing feature of the human neocortex. But recent research shows that there is possible asymmetry in the cortex of great apes (orangutan and chimpanzees).[1] Hemispheric asymmetry implies specialisation of function; coordination and integration therefore become critical. The size of the corpus callosum, a bundle of nerve-fibers connecting the right and left hemispheres, is consistent with the possibility of some hemispheric asymmetry for the great apes. This structure is relatively (and absolutely) large in humans, next in apes, then in monkeys, its volume (compared to the medulla) is 1.2 to 1 for monkeys, 1.8 to 1 for chimpanzees and 3 to 1 for humans.[2] In addition to investigating the anatomical bases, viewing communication in a social context with brain-behaviour interrelationships is an approach that will assist in integrating many types of data.

What is it about this paragraph that is distinctively academic in style? Certainly the content. And, linked with content, the use of specialist terms; for example, neocortex, corpus callosum. What else? Perhaps the cautiousness with which claims are made? 'But recent research shows ... *possible* asymmetry ...', 'The size of the corpus callosum ... is consistent with the *possibility* of ...'. The tone of the passage is very cool and detached. The writer is somewhat distanced from the material he is evaluating. Look too at the writer's concern for providing evidence, both within the text and through references, in support of the points he makes. This concern for evidence and objectivity of tone can lead to some very long and complex structures; look, for example, at the last sentence. Above all, there is a sense of a mind and voice moving steadily through the material: persuasive but distanced.

Consider the contrasting style of this passage:

Extract 2

I grant that high school classes are so large that marking for the teacher of English is a monstrous burden. But I believe strongly that there should be at least one written assignment marked every fortnight of the high school teaching year. I do not believe that poor expression should be left unmarked in case the mark scar the pupil's psyche. I believe excellence should be encouraged positively and ill-structured, ill-spelt, and ill-punctuated writing strongly discouraged. No football coach tolerates constantly muffed passes. Why should we grant less respect to man's greatest invention, language? And I mean greatest. You can take your nuclear reactors, your Pill and the sheer horror of having—in colour—the latest television 'personality' in your living room. These things are nothing, beside the magic fact that twenty-six symbols in various combinations on paper can reduce the reader to laughter or tears. I'm sentimental about language—the structure, the art of it. I find words endlessly entertaining. And when I taught primary and secondary levels, that was what I wanted my pupils to find, too.

How would you describe the tone of voice here? Is it cool and dispassionate, or emotional and strident? Objective or sensational? What justification are we given for believing in what the writer says? Are we offered evidence and reasoning, or simply unsupported assertion (polemic)? Is there anything distinctive about the vocabulary? Is there a tight logic in the development of ideas from the beginning to the end of the paragraph? In what context would we normally expect to find such sentences as 'And I mean the greatest. You can take your nuclear reactors ...'?

From this contrast you can recognise some characteristics of academic style. The academic writer's *approach* to his or her material is:

analytical		impressionistic
objective	*rather than*	subjective
intellectual		emotional
rational		polemical

The academic writer's *tone* is:

serious		conversational
impersonal	*rather than*	personal
formal		colloquial

The academic writer makes frequent use of:
passive forms of the verb
impersonal pronouns and phrases
qualifying words and phrases
complex sentence structures
specialised vocabulary

Check if you can identify some of these features of academic style in another passage; see Appendix 9.

In drawing attention to these characteristics of academic style, we are not suggesting that this is necessarily 'good' style. We are not saying, for example, that impersonal and passive forms, e.g. 'It may be inferred that . . .' are more effective than personal and active forms, e.g. 'I infer . . .' We are saying that the former are standard usage for much academic writing and therefore need to be learned and used when appropriate.

Differences between disciplines

So far we have isolated some of the common characteristics of academic style. You will soon realise, if you are studying in more than one discipline, that there are differences in style between disciplines as well as between academic and other forms of writing. Read the three following paragraphs and see if you can identify the disciplines from which they have been taken:

Extract 3

Exploratory tendencies evident in many animals seem also to reflect a preference for novelty or for increments in stimulation. Animals tend to explore actively any novel environment that permits more exploration over one that permits less. Moreover, animals will learn a response that is rewarded by the opportunity to explore. Rats choose the arm of a Y-maze that leads to a checkerboard maze over one that leads to a blind alley. Exploratory tendencies appear to be independent of general activity, and their occurrence does not require the accompanying state of deprivation that is characteristic of the regulatory drives such as hunger or thirst.

Extract 4
Our last example concerns the use of pronouns in BEV. Bereiter and Engelmann found that BEV speakers left out relative pronouns ('This here is one family eat nothing') but that they did use pronouns pleonastically ('My sister *she* play piano'). It is a part of their compensatory programme to adapt BEV children to the norms of pronoun use in SE. As Smith (1969) has already shown, however, such a measure would bring the child into verbal conflict. The reason for this is that there is a close correlation between the omission of the relative pronoun in BEV and the pleonastic use of the subject pronoun. In such sentences where the relative pronoun is omitted, the pleonastic pronoun is applied to remove any ambiguities. If, therefore, the programme of Bereiter and Engelmann is supposed to teach the children to omit the pleonastic pronoun, this will cause communicative interference within BEV usage.

Extract 5
But what one makes of the ending of the play depends on what one makes of the Duke; and I am embarrassed about proceeding, since the Duke has been very adequately dealt with by Wilson Knight, whose essay Knights refers to. The Duke, it is important to note, was invented by Shakespeare: in <u>Promos and Cassandra</u>, Shakespeare's source, there is no equivalent. He, his delegation of authority and his disguise (themselves familiar romantic conventions) are the means by which Shakespeare transforms a romantic comedy into a completely and profoundly serious 'criticism of life'. The more-than-Prospero of the play, it is the Duke who initiates and controls the experimental demonstration—the controlled experiment—that forms the action.

You may have been able to identify them as coming from the disciplines of psychology, linguistics (more exactly, sociolinguistics) and literary criticism respectively. There are a number of clues you may have used:

1 Content: Running rats through mazes to test behaviour patterns is a standard psychological experiment; the other two extracts are equally unambiguous in their content.

2 Vocabulary: Each discipline has its own technical language or jargon: 'drive', 'response', 'reward', 'stimulation' typically belong to psychological language (though they are also used, in different senses, in common speech); 'pleonastic pronouns', 'communicative interference', 'BEV' (Black English Vernacular) are part of the standard jargon of linguistics. Is there any jargon in Extract 5?

3 Special interests: Extract 5 is exploring the value or quality of the writing of Shakespeare and the justice of other writers' judgements upon him. This is the special interest of literary criticism. Extract 4 is not interested in questions of the aesthetic quality of language but in understanding in a scientific sense the way in which different groups in a community learn and use language. This is one of the special interests of sociolinguistics. What special interest is evident in Extract 3?

You might have noticed some other differences. Extract 5, for example, uses a *personal* form ('I am embarrassed . . .') whereas the other extracts do not. This personal usage is permissible in literary criticism in which there is a greater degree of reliance on subjective response as the basis of argument than in other disciplines. This is not to suggest that it is simply a matter of assertion of opinion. You will notice that the writer of Extract 5, in the same way as the writer of the sociolinguistic extract, is framing his argument in terms of other writers, critics or sources. Thus the writer measures his own response to the play against those of two other literary critics. All become part of the texture of the writer's own argument about the value of Shakespeare's writing. In a similar way, Smith's criticism of Bereiter and Engelmann is part of the sociolinguist's justification for his own argument. The same general academic method is at work in all the passages.

We started this section by asking: are the voice and style you adopt (i) appropriate, and (ii) consistent? We have tried to show what is 'appropriate' by sketching some common features of academic style and by pointing to some differences between disciplines. There is no quick or easy way of mastering these characteristics of style. That takes understanding, concentration, and a concern for detail — and it takes time. You will get better at it:

● the more you read in your disciplines
● the more you listen to lectures and take part in tutorials and seminars
● the more closely you attend to the criticisms and comments made on your essays and assignments

Summary

In this chapter we have tried to analyse what is involved in the central intellectual task of drafting and redrafting your essay. We have looked at some of the common problems which essay writers experience and suggested some strategies for overcoming them.

The important points to remember are:

1 You will need to write at least two drafts of each essay.

2 Your first draft is written for yourself, in order to establish exactly what you think; subsequent drafts are written for an external reader, and your material and style need to be tailored accordingly.

3 Your essay is the result of a balance struck between your own purposes in writing, your content, your reader's expectations, and the context in which you are writing.

4 You will need to develop strategies for overcoming those problems you experience in writing a first draft; for example, being unable to get started or losing the track of your argument.

5 Your redrafting should be based on two major questions:
Is the essay intellectually convincing?
Does it sound convincing?

6 You should apply to your own writing the criteria of logic and coherence at the paragraph level which were explored in the earlier chapter on reading. In particular, you should give attention to the special functions of the introductory and concluding paragraphs.

7 You should be aware of the characteristic features of academic style.

8 You should also be aware that there are differences in style and usage between disciplines.

*E*diting

Now you are ready to write out, or type, the final version
of your essay and hand it in. In this final writing you may
still be tinkering with a few sentences; trying to improve the
flow, emphasise a shift in thought, qualify a generalization.
But in general you will not now be making any substantial
changes or extensions to your argument. At this stage of
working on your essay a third question becomes important:

   Does it *look* convincing?

You are now working over your essay in the role of
editor or proof-reader, concerned with the surface presentation rather than the content. You may resent the necessity
to spend time on superficial details, especially after your
much weightier struggles with ideas and language. Yet
presentation is an important element in the persuasiveness of
your case. If there are signs of inaccuracy and carelessness at
the surface level of your essay, these will invite superficial
criticisms from your reader — and may well distract from a
more serious consideration of the real argument you have
struggled to present. This is the one stage in the whole
process of essay writing where there *is* only one way to be
'correct' and where the criteria for 'correctness' are objective
and are based on commonly accepted conventions and
practices.

In Chapter 6 we used a checklist to identify the main
points to be considered in the drafting stages of the essay.
The controlling questions in that checklist were:

   Is it *intellectually* convincing?
   Does it *sound* convincing?

The practical strategies you used there were largely matters
of *judgement*. In this final stage of editing, however, the

practical strategies involve strict application of rules and conventions. Now look over this checklist for the final editing stage.

Checklist for editing essays

Question: Does it *look* convincing?	Practical strategies for finding solutions
1 Have you observed the official departmental requirements for the *format* of the essay: • what size paper? • do you write on one side only? • what size margins? • if you are typing, should you use double-spacing? • what must be included on the title page? • is an abstract/synopsis/ summary required?	Reread the departmental handout on essay presentation and any particular instructions given for this essay.
2 Is your writing *correct* at the surface level of: • spelling? • punctuation? • grammar? Is it legible?	Read the essay carefully one final time, or ask a reliable friend to proofread it for you. Consult a dictionary or a standard reference book. (See Appendix 12 for a list of useful reference books.)
3 Are the *quotations* you have used: • accurate? • acknowledged? • correctly set out? • fully incorporated into the grammar of your own text?	Check any instructions in departmental handouts about the use of quotations. Read aloud the passages in your essay which include direct quotations and listen to see if they fit in smoothly. If you are unsure about how to handle quotations, see Appendix 13.
4 Are your *references* accurate and correctly set out?	Check departmental handouts. See Appendix 14 for some common referencing styles.

5 Is your *bibliography* accurate and correctly set out?	Check departmental handouts. A common model is provided in Appendix 15.
6 If a *synopsis* is required, is it in the correct style?	Reread instructions for essay. The art of constructing a synopsis/abstract/summary is discussed later in this chapter.

Practical strategies

Here are some additional comments on the checklist.

Essay format

1 Margins: It is important to leave margins which give your lecturer sufficient space in which to write comments as he or she reads your essay. If you do not, then you will be irritating your reader and you will not get feedback on the details of your work.

2 Title page: Some lecturers insist on a specific format for the cover or title page for your assignment: for example, it may be mandatory that you put your name on the back of the last page and not on the front page. If there are no instructions, then it is customary to include (in whatever format you find most pleasing):

- the essay title in full
- the name of the lecturer/tutor to whom you are submitting the essay
- the name of the course
- your own name.

Correct use of language

1 Spelling: If you know you are a weak speller, try to get a friend to read over your final draft and pencil in corrections. It is not 'cheating' to get editing assistance; just good sense. There may be ways in which you can improve your spelling ability, but you will almost certainly have exhausted these possibilities already in the earlier stages of your schooling. Some students find it useful to make lists of frequently misspelt words and stick them on the wall in front of their desk.

2 Expression: If your past essays have been criticised for 'awkward expression', it may help to read *aloud* your final draft. Many students find they can hear mistakes which they cannot pick up merely by looking at the written text.

You should also make a habit of consulting standard reference texts for grammar, punctuation and correct usage.

Quotations

1 Format and referencing: Whenever you copy a passage, word for word, from the work of some other writer, you are quoting. Then you must indicate the quotation by (i) using a special format (either inverted commas for a short quotation, or indentation for a quotation longer than three lines), and by (ii) giving an exact page reference to the source from which you have copied the passage. If you do not indicate quoted passages in this way, you may be accused of *plagiarism*, that is the unattributed use of the words and work of other writers.

2 Usage: There is no rule for when or how much you should quote. In some disciplines, such as literary criticism, you may need to quote constantly; in others it may be enough to summarize or make reference to a source. In general, check that your quotations are:

- used sparingly
- focused precisely on the point you are making
- brief and telling
- properly integrated into the flow of your argument and the grammar of your own sentences.

Once you have used a quotation, avoid restating it in your own words. The quotation must play its own part in advancing your argument.

References

In an essay, whenever you are:

- quoting the exact words of another writer,
- closely summarizing a passage from another writer,

- using an idea or material which is directly based on the work of another writer

then you must acknowledge your source. The three most common referencing styles for printed materials are:

1 Footnotes: numbers in the body of the text, following each reference, and numbered acknowledgements of the sources at the bottom of each page. This has the advantage of making it easy for the reader to identify a source at a glance.

2 Endnotes: numbers in the text but running consecutively throughout the whole essay, and the numbered acknowledgements given in a list at the end of the essay. This permits you to give extended commentaries and additional information about points in your essay.

3 Included references: The minimum information necessary to identify the source is given in brackets in the body of the essay: usually the author's name, date of publication and page number(s). Full details of the printed source are obtained through reference to the bibliography. This format is common in Science and the Social Sciences.

Bibliography

This is a list of all the printed sources you have found useful during your preparation for the essay — not merely a list of the sources you have actually referred to in the final essay. It is arranged alphabetically, by surname of author, and must have a consistent format.

In Science essays it is usual to give a list of **References** which contains only the sources you have actually cited in the body of your essay.

Synopsis

In some courses, especially in Science and the Social Sciences, you may be required to provide a synopsis (or abstract or summary). This should cover only the outline of your argument (not the details) and the general conclusions you have reached. If the length of the synopsis is not specified, it is usual to aim at a word total of approximately 5–10 per cent of the length of the essay itself.

The synopsis is placed following the title page and in front of the actual essay, so that your reader can see in advance the whole sweep of your argument and the conclusions which you are going to present.

In fact you will write your synopsis *after* you have completed your essay. It is a summary of what you have written, not a blueprint of what you intend to write. For this reason it is customary to write the summary in the present, not the future, tense.

Many academic journals require writers to provide a synopsis or abstract at the head of their article and you can find plenty of examples merely by leafing through journals in your discipline. Here is an example taken from the British Journal of Psychology ([1966] **57**, 3 and 4, p. 361):

Transfer in Category Learning of Young Children: Its Relation to Task Complexity and Overlearning

By Ann M. Clarke and G.M. Cooper
Department of Psychology, The University of Hull

An investigation with normal pre-school children is reported which confirms and extends earlier findings on subnormal subjects. That transfer is related to the complexity of intervening is again demonstrated across widely different tasks. In addition, evidence is offered for the interaction of overlearning with complexity, and the possible relevance of transfer in cognitive development is briefly discussed.

And here is an example of a synopsis by a student in a Sociology course:

The work of Hargreaves and Willis provides a framework for examining two factors which contribute to deviant behaviour among English school children. First, the structure of the school system, which is strongly oriented towards achievement, works against low achievers. Second, the essentially middle-class value system of the teachers is in conflict with the essentially oppositional culture of working-class pupils. It is argued that the development of closer links between the school and industry (the end to which school is leading for the majority of working-class pupils) might lead to adjustments in both school ethos and pupils' behaviour. A more effective and acceptable form of secondary education might follow from such adjustments.

Wordprocessing

Many students are now writing their essays and reports on computers. The advantages of wordprocessing are obvious: you can rewrite parts of your essay that you are unhappy with easily and quickly; you can shift whole blocks of material around if you don't like the initial organization of your ideas; you can apply a range of programmed aids and checks (such as Spellcheck) to what you have written; and you can edit and polish your language to your heart's content — without the bother of having to retype whole pages for perfect presentation.

But all new technologies bring problems as well as benefits. There are two very common pitfalls with wordprocessing. First, some writers have a tendency to become mesmerized by their screens. Thus they produce essays with paragraphs all of the same size, not because their argument or material requires such conformity but because their paragraphs have been shaped to correspond exactly with the size of the screen.

Second, and relatedly, some writers are tempted to polish and perfect single paragraphs (often the opening ones) rather than getting on with the job of developing the whole essay. Having polished and perfected these single paragraphs, they are then reluctant to make the changes that are needed once the draft is complete.

Our advice is that is it usually better to push on and complete the draft, then print out and do your editing on the hard copy before you enter the changes into the machine. It is vitally important for the structure and coherence of your essay that you see the whole essay as one piece and not just as it rolls past your eye or in separate screenfuls of print.

Summary

In this chapter we have provided a practical checklist to cover those aspects of your final draft which need special attention in editing.

The main points to remember are:

1 Your final essay must be as accurate as possible in details of presentation.

2 You should always check the specific requirements of the department about essay presentation.

3 You should know how to handle quotations, referencing of sources, format for bibliographies, and other requirements of presentation.

4 You may find it useful to ask a friend to read over the final version of your essay in order to pick up errors.

5 If you are writing on a computer, write a complete draft before polishing, and print out the essay so that you can analyse the coherence of the whole.

8

Assessment and follow-up

At last it's finished. Your essay has been handed in, and there is nothing more you can do about it. You may simply feel relieved — 'I just couldn't do any more with it.' 'I was sick to death of it.' 'I just wanted to get rid of it.' 'Once I'd submitted it, I felt as if a great weight had been lifted off my back.' Or your relief may be tinged with anxiety — 'I know it's not perfect, but I think it's more or less all right.' 'What mark will I get?' 'It's only when I get it back that I'll know how good it was, how good the lecturer thought it was.' Yet is this the end of the whole process? What more can you learn from what you have done? There is more to assessment than the final grade.

There are three points at which you can start analysing how effectively you handled the process of writing in that essay:

- the formal assessment by your lecturer
- your self-assessment
- discussion with other students.

Feedback from lecturers

The formal assessment of your work may be of three kinds: letter grade or numerical mark; written comments; and direct discussion.

1 Grade or mark: Your immediate reaction, on getting back your essay, is probably to look first for the grade it was given. This represents the 'official' judgement on your performance and is an evaluation both of the quality of your work and the way in which it compares with the work of other students. Of course, this grade is not the final judgement on your intellectual capacities; but it is some indication of your current performance.

2 Written comments: Most commonly your lecturer will write comments on your essay, as well as giving you a final grade. There will be comments in the margin, mainly concerned with details at the sentence level, and a more extended end comment focusing on the whole essay and possibly suggesting strategies for improvement in the next essay.

Let us look at an example of each type of comment. First, here is a paragraph from an English essay on a scene from Macbeth. The essay was written by a first-year student and commented on in detail by the marker:

Macbeth, when he learns that Fleance 'is scaped' (line 18) and hence that he has not forestalled the witches' second prophesy, is '...cabined, cribbed, confinded, bound in/To saucy doubts and fears.'

You must be more specific.

(lines 23–24), the tone, rhythdm and imagery which the words create show clearly what he is thinking, and they also tell his character and how he

which is ?.

can be trapped by his own thoughts. There is also, in this scene a contrast between Macbeth's apparently orderly front when he is trying to make his Lords feel all is well and the turmoil his mind is in when the ghost appears, this seems to make one feel that Macbeth is really in the grip of something he cannot

In combination with his ambition, his vulnerability to the supernatural and his wife's initial manipulations.

control. And so perhaps the ghost, although it may be real, is made more real, a horribly powerful and disorderly force, by Macbeth's own fretted mind. It is this aspect of his character which seems to be his downfall; his mind is a prey to his imagination. With 'Which of you has done this' (line 47) when he sees the ghost for the first time he becomes divorced

I don't see the connection between your quotation and your assertion

from the present, perhaps from reality, and totally absorbed in the horror of his deeds and the *effect?* supernatural which has such a destructive force on

You should organize material more effectively

him. As the ghost itself exits and enters, dramatic effectiveness is built up not only on stage but also in *and?* the audience, one feels pulled into the action.

instead of commenting on dramatic effectiveness at this point, you ought to continue discussing Macbeth's state of mind.

And here is an example of detailed end comment on a first-year essay in European Literature and Society (1789–1850):

Topic: Is <u>Scarlet and Black</u> a story of success or failure?

Comment: An old but still quite reliable rule for the construction of a discussion or argument is that it should have three identifiable sections: an introduction; a development; and a conclusion.

This essay seems to me to have an approximation of those three parts. However, it is only the conclusion that is really recognisable as what it should be. And a conclusion that is preceded by a sketchy and unfocused introduction, and by a development that never comes to grips with the matter supposedly under discussion, can never be anything but a good intention.

Let your introduction be two things: a definition of terms; and a blueprint of the discussion to follow, the shape of the argument. In this topic, there are, it seems to me, two terms that should be clarified from the outset: success and failure. Each of these terms can bear at least two meanings: success and failure as judged by the world at large; and the same things as judged by the self. It is the paradox of this ambiguity that your introduction should have tried to clear up. In so doing, you would inevitably have had to pass on to your reader a hint about what shape your essay was going to take e.g. 'Having defined my terms as etc. etc., I now propose to examine the first of these terms etc. etc...' The reader would have had a clue about the trend of your argument before you get into it; and that is a great advantage to both you and your reader.

Your development: you have written a fairly thorough, very accurate, summary of the events that make up the plot of the novel. However, plot is not theme. And it is the theme of success/failure, as presented by Stendhal through the events, that you should have been examining.

It is obvious that you *see* the difference between Julien's public failure and private failure; but nowhere do you focus your mind on it and write the few paragraphs of discussion that it calls for. The theme is implicit in what you say and in the quotations which you choose from the text of the novel. But it should be explicit; otherwise there is no discussion of the evidence, merely the evidence presented as though it was self-explanatory.

A smaller point: when recounting plot, use the present tense; it is the usual thing. And pay attention to using the same tense all the time.

Notice my suggestion on page 3 about a better way to make sentences. If you write shorter sentences, if you teach yourself to pause and think of some other word every time you feel tempted to link clauses with *ands* and *buts*, then you will probably write more clearly and intelligently.

Notice, too, that some of your punctuation could improve.

Misspelling of proper names is a form of vermin; it should be stamped out by the simple device of checking them in the text.

As you can see from both sets of comments, the lecturer is conducting a discussion with the student, and there is an underlying assumption that the argument expressed in the essay is still open to further refinement and that the method or presentation can still be improved. These comments become part of the continuous process of learning; a further step, rather than a dead end.

3 Personal discussion: In some cases your lecturer may arrange to hand back your essay to you personally or ask you to come and discuss it individually at a later time. Although such an interview may seen daunting at first, it is often the most helpful form of feedback you can get. It gives you a chance to explain your ideas more thoroughly and to talk about more effective ways of presenting them. You can also ask your lecturer to explain in more detail the criticisms made of your essay.

Self-assessment

It is useful to judge your own essay on two grounds:

- What are the strengths and weaknesses of *what you did produce?*
- What are the strengths and weaknesses of *the way in which you worked* on the essay?

1 What did you produce? In judging your own work you will inevitably be influenced by the formal assessment you received. In fact you may find you disagree with some of the lecturer's criticisms even after you have considered them as objectively as you can. For example, the lecturer may have criticized your interpretation of a source or incident, but you may remain convinced that it does have the significance you have attributed to it. Well, there is no law that you must agree with everything your lecturer thinks. One lesson you might draw is that next time you must manage to present your views more convincingly.

It can be helpful to list separately:

- the comments which bear on the *subject matter* of the essay — questions of fact, accuracy, evidence, sources, etc.
- the comments which bear on your *use* of your material — choice of quotations, analysis of different approaches, your conclusions, etc.
- the comments which bear on the *surface features* of your presentation — spelling, referencing format, etc.

You will then be in a position to plan your strategies for the writing of your next essay more clearly.

2 How did you work? In order to improve your working strategies, it might be helpful to ask yourself these questions:

- How efficient were my reading strategies:
    Did I spend too much time on general materials?
    Did I miss an important source?
- How useful were my notes:
    Did they cover much more material than I needed?
    Did they leave out essential details about sources?
    Were they easy to reorganize into a structure for the essay?
- Was the time I spent on thinking and planning well spent:
    Should I have spent more or less time on this stage?
    How representative of the final essay was my original outline plan?
- Did I start the writing stage too soon, or too late?
- Are there ways I might have cut down on the redrafting and editing stages, or should I have allowed more time for these?

Discussion with other students

A final, and often neglected, strategy is to discuss your work with fellow students. If you can persuade a small group of friends to swop essays, this is a most useful pooling of resources. It may be a difficult procedure to get started, but it can help you to understand the qualities of thinking and writing which constitute a good essay and the variety of ways in which the same task can be tackled.

Summary

In this short chapter we have suggested that the assessment of your completed essay is an essential stage in the continuous process of learning. Through analysing the response of your lecturer to your essay, through evaluating your own methods of writing, and by comparing your essay and ideas with those of other students, you can improve your future performance.

The main points to remember are:

1 It is important to understand *why* your lecturer commented upon and graded your essay as he or she did.

2 Discussion of your work with your lecturer and with other students is often the most useful source of feedback.

9

Writing reviews and reports

So far we have talked about writing essays — the most common type of written assignment that you will meet in your courses. But you may also encounter some more specialised types of assignment such as book reviews and research reports which present additional demands to those we have discussed already. Some requirements remain constant, of course, no matter whether you are writing essays, reviews or reports. In all cases, for example, you are expected to think critically about your content. Similarly, you must still analyse and present that content in such a way that your reader is persuaded of the force of your conclusion or evaluation. But your lecturers will have particular expectations about the style and format of reviews and reports, and you will need to be aware of the nature of these expectations.

Here we will look very briefly at three special types of assignments:

the book review;
the research lab report; and
the fieldwork report.

Book review

In later year courses you may be asked to write a book review; often this is the first written assignment set in a course. A close and critical reading of a book provides a good introduction to a new topic or to the theoretical base of the discipline or to the current state of knowledge in the field. The purpose of such a review is not, as in reviews in newspapers, merely to highlight the key features of the book in such a way that your reader will be encouraged to rush off and buy it for Christmas. Here your review is being written for a reader (your lecturer) who is already knowledgeable in the discipline. Your lecturer is not so much interested in whether you can summarize the content of the book as in whether you can critically assess the quality of the ideas, the data and the arguments being presented by the author.

In most cases your review will have to answer some or all of the following questions:

- Is this an important book (within the discipline)? Why or why not?
- What range of material does it cover?
- What theoretical approach is used in presenting this material?
- What are the particular strengths and weaknesses of the author's discussion?
- What is your overall evaluation of this book, and for what reasons?

If you turn to Appendix 10, you will find examples of book review assignments from two different disciplines which indicate the specific purposes the lecturers had in mind when they set these tasks.

Writing the review

Step 1 Get a feel of the book you have selected to review by using your skimming skills:

- Glance at the title, table of contents, and the Preface or Introduction. These should give you some idea of the coverage of the book and its method of organization and, if the Preface is useful, also the author's reason for writing.
- Skim quickly through the whole book, running your eye over headings and sub-headings and over opening sentences of paragraphs. Look quickly at any tables, illustrations or other graphic materials. This should confirm and extend your initial impression of the scope and focus of the author's work.
- Read more closely the first chapter. This will usually set out the main issues to be discussed and indicate the theoretical or conceptual framework within which the author proposes to work.

- Read closely the final chapter, which should cover the author's conclusions and summarise the main reasons why these conclusions have been reached.

Step 2 Now you must go back and read the book in more detail, and decide which aspects you wish to discuss in your review. Maybe you think the most important part is the theoretical approach, or the data presented, or a particular case study used, or the author's selection and interpretation of evidence, or the range of coverage, or the style of presentation. At this stage you will be taking notes, identifying key quotations and so gathering your own data from your source. Nearly always you will choose to discuss the issues the author has identified as being important, but sometimes you may want to concentrate on a relatively minor point in the book because it is a central point in the course you are studying. In any case you are beginning to shape your own review by the decisions you make at this stage.

Step 3 Depending on the length of your review, you may want to read other articles or chapters of books to find supporting evidence or different models or alternative interpretations of data to those presented by your author. You may also want to glance at (but not reproduce) reviews of the book in recent academic journals. Apart from providing you with a model for academic book reviews, this additional reading will give you some feel for the way the book has been received within the discipline. In this way you will become better informed about the general field of study and more confident in your own evaluation of the particular work you are reviewing.

Step 4 You are now ready to start drafting your assignment. The structure of the review should include:

- an *initial identification* of the book (author, date, title, publisher) and an indication of the major aspects of the book you will be discussing;
- a *brief summary* of the range, contents and argument of the book. Occasionally you may need to summarise chapter by chapter but in a short review you usually pick out the main themes only. Here you also point out the theoretical perspective or viewpoint from which the book is written. (This section would normally take up about a third of your total review);

- a *critical discussion* of 2–3 key issues raised in the book. This section is the core of your review. You need to make clear the author's own argument and evidence before you criticize and evaluate it. And you must support your criticisms with evidence from the text or from other writings. You may want to indicate gaps in the author's treatment of a topic, but it is seldom useful to criticize writers for not doing something they never intended or claimed to do; and
- a *final evaluation* of the overall contribution this book has made to your understanding of the topic (and, maybe, its importance to the development of the discipline, setting it in the context of other writings in the field).

Appendix 10 also includes a brief checklist which you may find useful when you are writing the final draft of your review.

Research lab report

In many Science courses you are required to write regular lab reports which follow a format set out in your lab manual and are very similar to those you learned to write in school. However in some courses, such as Psychology, you may be asked to write a lab report which is, in fact, much more like an article in an academic journal — indeed the prescribed format is often copied from a leading journal in the discipline. This can be a tricky task until you become familiar with the style and format that are expected.

In Appendix 12 we refer to a book on scientific writing by David Lindsay which you may find helpful when writing such reports.

Your report will normally be divided into four sections (together with a Bibliography or list of References you have cited in your report, and maybe some Appendices for additional data):

Introduction: Here you justify the need for and design of your research project. You have to show how it fits into the main field of inquiry and how it derives from previous research. The normal way to do this is to refer to the major research studies which are relevant to your investigation (in longer reports this is commonly known as a literature review). You will have to discuss the links and the gaps in the previous research in order to show the intention underlying your own study or experiment. Is it merely replicating someone else's study to verify their results? Or is it actually intended to clarify a problem that your discussion of previous research has highlighted? Maybe it is designed to fill some gap in the research record, or to take the research one step further? This underlying intention must then be made clear in the final paragraph of your Introduction where you set out, in very concise form, the aims or hypotheses of your project.

Materials and methods: In this section you set out all the details of your sample, your research design and methodology, and the instruments you used in your study. The information you provide should be detailed enough to allow your reader to follow or repeat your experiment.

Results: Here you present the results of your investigation in quantitative form, usually in tables and usually with statistical applications. Each table must be clearly headed with all the relevant information about subjects and scales of measurement necessary for a full interpretation of the data. You usually have to summarize the main points of each table in words, drawing attention to any significant findings. Such findings become the subject of discussion in the final section of your report. If you are asked to submit all your raw data (ie before they have been categorized into separate tables or submitted to statistical analysis), you can do this in an appendix to the report.

Discussion: You should start this section by immediately showing the relationship of your findings to your original aims or hypotheses, as stated at the end of your Introduction. You need then to discuss the significance of your findings and comment on unexpected variations or contradictions in your results. In doing this you will probably find yourself drawing on some of the studies you referred to in your Introduction. It is common to conclude a report by suggesting improvements or variations that should be made in any further research on this topic.

In Appendix 11 you will find a convenient checklist against which you can assess the final draft of your lab report before you submit it.

Fieldwork report

In some courses, maybe Geography, Environmental Studies, or Sociology, you might be asked to do some fieldwork and then write it up in the form of a report. Depending on the course, you may have to record data collected via a survey or some other form of measurement. This material then becomes the basis of your report, and your main task is two-fold:

- you have to present the data you have collected; and
- you must offer some interpretation of its significance.

Fieldwork reports tend to be more flexible and varied in structure than the tightly controlled lab report described above. Nevertheless the fieldwork report is a variant on the lab report rather than a totally separate species of writing, and you will usually find that such reports have a common underlying structure:

Title
Introduction (including Aim)
Methods (where applicable)
Presentation of data
Discussion
Conclusion
Bibliography or References
Appendices (where applicable).

Normally your lecturer will provide guidelines on matters of structure and format: you may, for example, be asked to provide an abstract in addition to what is laid out above or, if your report is very long, a table of contents.

Apart from the general headings suggested above, fieldwork reports tend to make frequent use of sub-headings and sub-divisions, and the data are often presented in graphic or tabular form, either in the body of the report or in appendices. The guiding principle for these reports is that you are looking for a structure and format which will allow you to present your information, and the interpretation of that information, as clearly as possible to your reader.

Summary

In this chapter we have looked at some writing tasks which have very specific requirements in terms of structure and format: the book review, the research lab report, and the fieldwork report. They all require critical and analytical thought, and the logical development of an argument or point of view is still basic to such assignments though less obvious than in a conventional essay.

The main points to remember are:

1 It is important to follow the guidelines set out by your lecturer or modelled in the relevant academic journal.

2 Your writing should focus on your data, whether in the form of a book or research findings, and you must draw your conclusions largely from that material.

10

*E*xam essays

So, you've learnt to write essays. You've learnt to spend time analysing an essay topic, reading around the subject, gradually working your way into an understanding of what is required, redrafting your initial writing, clarifying your ideas and argument.

But you will need to change some of these methods of working if you are to handle exam essays competently.

Change what? The way in which you prepare. The speed at which you work. Your ways of actually planning and writing an exam answer. In the exam room, limited time and lack of source materials will force you to make these changes to your pattern of working. Nonetheless, you will find that those skills and habits which you have already developed in writing term essays are also important for exam essays. The whole process of essay writing will be speeded up, but the intellectual tasks are similar.

Your efficiency in an exam will depend to a great extent on the effectiveness of your preparation. And a good way to start your revision is to think about the differing expectations of your lecturers about exam essays in contrast to term essays.

Expectations

Lecturers' expectations about term essays (see Ch. 1)	Lecturers' expectations about exam essays
1 It is expected that your essay will be clearly focused on the set topic and will deal fully with its central concerns (p. 4).	**1** The same, except 'deal fully' will imply 'as fully as possible within the limits of the exam time'.

Lecturers' expectations about term essays (see Ch. 1)	Lecturers' expectations about exam essays
2 It is expected that your essay will be the result of wide and critical reading (p. 6).	**2** Your essay will be the result of systematic revision of the materials used in the course.
3 It is expected that your essay will present a reasoned argument (p. 8).	**3** The same, though your exam essay is not expected to be as well-structured because there is little time for redrafting.
4 It is expected that your essay will be competently presented (p. 10).	**4** Less important, except possibly the legibility of your handwriting.

Identifying probable exam topics

How can you set about revising effectively when you don't know what the exam will be about? It's certainly a problem, but there are ways in which you can start to identify the topics which will *probably* be set. You can never be certain that a particular topic will turn up, and you will have almost no clues as to the precise wording and focus of the actual questions on the paper. However, you can narrow the range of topics with some confidence.

Here are three ways in which you might start this process:

1 Look at past exam papers. These are useful, but never sure, guides. There may have been a change of lecturer, or of some of the course content, or of the style and format of the exam (for example, a shift from three essays to three short answers and a multiple-choice section).

Initially your purpose in skimming past exam papers is to:

- *identify the main topics* which are covered. For example, is there usually a question on kinship in the Anthropology exam? Or on meteorology in the Geography paper?
- become familiar with the *format* of the exam. For example, how many questions are set, and within what time limits? Is the paper divided into sections? Are any sections compulsory?

2 Use any departmental sources which you can find to clarify your understanding of the content of the course and, therefore, of the probable scope of the exam paper. Departmental handouts and the course outline in the Faculty Handbook should give you a brief summary of the aims and content of the course. This can help you to identify both the key concepts and issues which have been covered during the year and the rationale underlying the whole course.

3 Read through all your lecture notes and tutorial notes, both to refresh your memory of the whole sweep of the course and to identify the main divisions into which the course falls.

Now you should be in a position to pick out the specific topics you want to concentrate on in your revision.

Reading and other revision activities

In your reading for a term essay you are trying to find relevant sources and extend your understanding of the topic. In revising for exams, by contrast, you are trying to consolidate and clarify the knowledge you have already acquired. So your study strategies must change. Revision must be an active process in which you rework and rethink your materials in a variety of ways.

Here are some suggestions:

1 Make *summaries* of your notes as you read and try to *condense* a whole section of the course into a page or two of notes. In this way you are forcing yourself to identify key points. These points, recombined in new ways to meet the specific demands of your exam questions, will be as much material as you can handle in the exam time. These summaries also have the advantage that they can be used effectively in the final stages of your revision when you are desperately trying to remind yourself of everything you should already know. They can give you confidence that the task is manageable.

2 Check your revision notes against *past exam papers*:

- which questions relate to the material you have been revising?

- what points would you need to cover in order to answer each question?

3 You can also try framing *your own exam questions* based on the materials you are revising.

(These three strategies are particularly valuable if you are working in a study group. The comments, insights and different approaches of other students can help to sharpen your own ideas.)

4 You may also find it useful to write a *trial answer* to one question, without looking at your revision notes and within the time limit of the exam. Some lecturers and tutors are willing to skim through these trial efforts and comment on your performance. Other students may be helpful in suggesting ways in which you could have handled the topic more effectively. And even if you can get no outside feedback, this exercise is still useful in demonstrating just how much — or how little — you can write on a question within the limited time.

5 In some courses you may be allowed to take notes and other materials into the exam room. However, you'll need to organise these materials beforehand so that you can use them quickly and efficiently within the exam time limits.

Planning and writing

Exams demand a quick response; but also a response that is accurately directed to the terms of the set question. You may find it helpful to keep these three steps in mind as you start your actual exam:

1 Once you have chosen the questions you will answer, make notes for each (on the exam paper, on rough paper, anywhere) on the points, facts, names, dates and other relevant information which immediately come to mind. Later these first responses must be reorganised coherently, but they can be very helpful both in starting your mind working and in assisting you to switch your concentration to the next question as soon as you have completed one answer.

2 Before you start planning each answer, look closely at the wording of the question. Make quite sure that you have understood the content you must cover and the way in which you are directed to use it.

3 Plan your answer as clearly as possible *before* you start writing.

By comparison with term essay writing, the exam allows you the opportunity for *only one draft*. Inevitably this will result in a rougher presentation: there may be awkward links between one point and the next; the direction of your argument may shift; you may remember points late in your essay which should have appeared earlier; the introduction and conclusion may not be very polished. To some extent your examiner will make allowances for these shortcomings. On the other hand, those exam answers which exhibit the qualities of a good essay will be appreciated.

Editing

Editing (if it takes place at all) is a very hasty process in exams. It is commonplace advice that you allow five minutes (or more) at the end of each exam answer for editing. In practice, if you do have time to spare, certainly go back over your answers to correct errors of fact, style and grammar. However, in many exams you will find you have little time, or taste, for rereading what you have written. You must rely on the fluent style and the habits of accuracy and clarity which you have been consciously developing over the year's work.

Summary

In this final chapter we have discussed some of the adaptations you must make to your essay-writing methods when you are handling exam essays. The most significant differences arise from the constraints on time and access to source materials. Efficient revision is the basis for effective exam answers.

The main points to remember are:

1 In your exam essays you should aim for the same qualities as in your term essays, though your answers will probably be less competently argued and less polished.

2 You should begin your revision by trying to identify the topics on which exam questions will probably be based.

3 Good revision is an active process in which you rework your material so that it can be used with flexibility and efficiency in the exam.

4 Working in a study group is a particularly useful strategy for revision.

5 In the exam you should analyse and plan each answer clearly before you start writing it.

6 Your approach to exam essays and your success in handling them will reflect the competence you have developed in essay writing throughout the whole course.

Appendices

Appendix 1

Practice in analysing a reading list (see Chapter 3, page 21)

Look at the following topic and related reading list which were given to students in a Prehistory course. Following the suggestions made in Chapter 3, analyse the list in relation to the set topic in order to decide:

- what you can learn from the reading list about the content and tasks involved in the essay;
- which might be the best books or articles to read initially.

You might also consider why the lecturer has recommended an article written in 1890, and why an article on an orangutan might be relevant to the essay topic.

Topic: What can we learn from experimental replication of stone artefacts?

Reading list:
Binford, S.R. & L.R. (1969), 'Stone tools and human behaviour', Scientific American, **220**, no. 4, pp. 70–84.
Coles, J.M. (1973), Archaeology by Experiment, Hutchinson.
Crabtree, D. (1972), 'An introduction to flintworking', Occ. Papers of Idaho State Museum, no. 28.
Holmes, W.H. (1890), 'A quarry workshop of the flaked-stone implement makers in the District of Columbia', American Anthropologist, **3**, pp. 1–26.
Semenov, S.A. (1964), Prehistoric Technology, Cory, Adams & Mackay.
Wright, R.V.S. (1972), 'Imitative learning of a flaked stone technology—The case of an orangutan', Mankind, **8**, pp. 296–306.

Appendix 2

Practice in skimming for understanding (see Chapter 3, page 38)

Step 1: Skim section 5 of the Beckett chapter by reading only the first sentences of each paragraph.

Step 2: Here are the sentences you have just read quickly:

The decisive influence of the Great Famine on the economic and social life of Ireland arose directly from the sudden and continuing decline in the population: it was an effective, though terrible, solution to the problem of rural over-crowding.

The change in the distribution of land had important social consequences.

Politically, as well as economically and socially, the famine had a profound influence on later developments.

The British attitude to Ireland, as well as the Irish attitude to Britain, was affected by the famine.

When, in August 1849, the queen made her first visit to Ireland she was welcomed with enormous popular enthusiasm; but it would be a mistake to regard this enthusiasm as a true indication of Irish feelings towards Britain, and it certainly had no lasting effect on British feelings towards Ireland.

Step 3: Even if some of these sentences are not fully clear to you (for example, you might be puzzled by the reference to changes in British attitudes to Ireland), can you still begin to understand the content and the argument of this section?

Step 4: Now read the whole section in full, noting how long this takes you.

Step 5: Consider the advantages you gained from the full reading (more information; a fuller understanding of the passage) and weigh these against the advantages of your previous skimming.

There is no 'right' conclusion to be reached — the point is to recognize the advantages and limitations of skimming so that you can make use of the skill when you think it is appropriate.

Appendix 3

Practice in skimming for an essay topic (see Chapter 3, page 41)

1 Assume that you have been set the essay topic:

'Starvation was only one consequence of the Great Famine, and not the most serious either.' Discuss.

2 Skim the whole Beckett extract in order to identify the material you think will be relevant to this topic.

3 Think over the following questions:

- How long, approximately, has this taken you?
- Which parts of the chapter would you need to reread more fully?
- If you compare the sections of the chapter which are relevant for this essay topic with the sections which were important for the essay you worked on in Chapter 3 (p. 42), what can you deduce about the content and task of each essay?
- Can you identify areas which you would need to cover in this essay which are not covered in the Beckett chapter?
- Would you organize your essay in the same way that Beckett has presented his material in this chapter?

Appendix 4

Modifications of skimming: an example (see Chapter 3, page 42)

Look at the following extract from a Psychology text and try skimming in the normal fashion, by reading *only* the first sentence of each paragraph.

I.Q. and age

As has been said, the ability to pass increasingly difficult items on intelligence tests grows rapidly during the years from birth to about the mid-teens—and particularly in the earliest years of childhood. This fact leads to some interesting questions: At what age does the kind of ability measured by intelligence tests reach its peak? Once the peak is attained, does the ability then decline during the middle and old age?

The answers to these questions are not easy to obtain, because they are complicated by the probability, which has just been mentioned, that the average score on intelligence tests has been rising generation by generation in recent years. If one were to administer the same kind of intelligence test to large numbers of people from teenagers to sixty-year-olds, one would naturally expect the younger people to make higher average scores than the older people—and this is indeed what has been found to happen.

For example, in standardizing a recent version of the Wechsler Adult Intelligence Scale, the test was administered to representative samples of various age groups from sixteen through sixty-four, and the results were as illustrated in Graph 1. Note that the average total score rose through the early twenties, remained more or less on a plateau until thirty-four, then began a fairly sharp and steady decline. However, the age-by-age patterns differed for the two parts of the test, the verbal items and the performance items. Ability at verbal skills, after reaching its peak between twenty-five and thirty-four, remained fairly constant

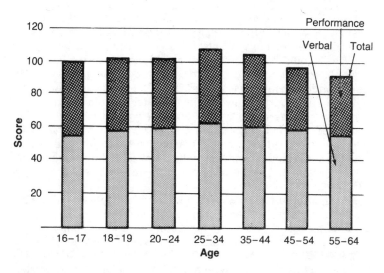

Graph 1 I.Q. by age groups Various age groups make different scores on the Wechsler Adult Intelligence Scale; the differences are apparent in both the verbal and performance parts of the test and in the total score as well. For a discussion of these results, see the text.

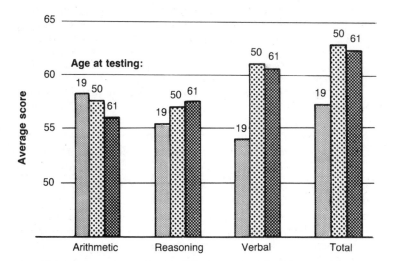

Graph 2 At what age are we smartest? The bars show the scores (not I.Q.'s) for three of the skills measured by an intelligence test, as well as the total score, made by men who were first tested when they were nineteen-year-old college freshmen, again when they were fifty, and a third time when they were sixty-one.

through the age of forty-four and afterward showed only a relatively small decline. Ability on performance items began to decline after the early twenties and at a fairly rapid rate.

What would be the results of a study in which the very same people could be tested over the years, beginning in their teens and continuing into their sixties? Despite the difficulties of making such a study, fortunately one investigator has managed to compare the scores made on a group intelligence test by nearly a hundred men during the First World War, when they were college freshmen averaging nineteen years old, with their scores on the same kind of test taken when they were fifty years old and again when they were sixty-one. The results are illustrated in Graph 2.

As the figure shows, scores on the arithmetic items in the test were highest at the age of nineteen and went down steadily thereafter. Scores on items measuring reasoning ability did just the opposite; they rose steadily and were highest at sixty-one. Scores on items measuring verbal ability were substantially higher at fifty than at nineteen but then declined slightly at sixty-one. The total score rose markedly from nineteen to fifty and afterward showed a slight decline. The results are not entirely satisfactory because they are for men only — and for a group that had an above-average I.Q. at first testing and presumably led lives more favorable than average to continued intellectual growth. However, they do offer a strong indication that intelligence — at least as measured by present tests — is by no means the monopoly of the young and that there is hardly any cause for despair over what will happen to our mental abilities as we get older.

---

from J. Kagan & E. Havemann (1968), Psychology: An Introduction, Harcourt, Brace, Jovanovich, Inc., New York, pp. 432–4.

You probably have found that skimming this passage by opening sentences does not yield any sensible structure. For example, the opening sentence of the second paragraph ('The answers to these questions are not easy to obtain . . .') can only be understood if you look back to the 'questions' which occur at the end of the previous paragraph. Similarly, the clue to the meaning of the first sentence in paragraph 5 ('As the figure shows . . .') lies in the final sentence of the fourth paragraph. However, once you have recognised the way in which the argument is organised, you can adapt your skimming procedure to take advantage of the structure; in this example you would probably skim both the first *and* final sentences of each paragraph. Similarly, if a writer tends to use first sentences as bridges, then you would focus quickly on the two opening sentences of each paragraph.

Appendix 5

Essay plans: examples
(see Chapter 3, page 56)

Here are plans developed by three students in a first-year Geography course. The students were required to write a 1500 word essay on the following topic:

'Urban planning in Britain since 1940 has improved the nature of cities in that country.'
Discuss this statement with particular reference to the planning of London.

All three used the same four books as sources:

R. Goodman, After the Planners, Penguin, 1972.
P. Hall, The World Cities, World Univ. Library, 1966.
_____ Urban and Regional Planning, Penguin, 1977 (rev. edn).
H. Stretton, Urban Planning in Rich and Poor Countries, OUP, 1978.

On the basis of their reading and what they learnt in lectures, they all reached the same general conclusion:

Yes, urban planning has improved the structure of London; but its effect on the quality of life and social objectives in the city is less certain.

The essay plans they produced, however, were very different. Anna, the student in Chapter 5 who claimed she tries to 'block out on a piece of paper the main points I want to make' and also notes likely quotes and references, produced the outline shown on page 118.

Ben, on the other hand, who explained his method of developing a series of increasingly detailed outlines, produced highly systematic plan shown on page 119.

'*Urban planning* in Britian, since 1940, has improved ~~how~~ far??'

define the nature of cities? in that country.' Discuss – re.

planning of London.

* ── *

Intro – Stretton quote re 'complicated' mod. city (p.10)

– re London (nb. main Reports) → struct. change/

also "nature"/?

urban

Style of /planning

Gout > private enterprise (Goodman)

– '40 Barlow, '44 Aberc., '47 S.E. System

Green belt → New Towns/ 'home & neighbourhood'

(Stret. p 104)

Nature of cities /London

① Pop. density

② Services

③ industry

get stats/tables
from Hall (p. 54)

Nb. white collar employ

Plans – slums /decentralize /but concent.

– Commuter belt   services in L.

RESULTS 1. old problems transf. to NTs

dev. etc.

2. quality of life – transport,

pollution

new problems

Concl. Yes, but no !!!

'Urban planning in Britain since 1940 has improved the nature of cities in that country.' Discuss this statement with particular reference to the planning of London.

Introduction: ·Structure of cities improved significantly —
but not social planning/quality of life/welfare.

1. Brief background: pressures for planning and change
   — postwar baby boom: 66 mil. by end of century
   — pop. segmenting into smaller and smaller households
   — increasing mobility
   — inter-regional migration to London and South
   — rising prosperity, eg cars, bigger houses (Hall 156f.)

2. Changes in structure (focus on London)

   (a) Legislation - 1945 Abercrombie's Greater London P. (based
       Barlow '40) —→ 30 miles London ring,
       decentralization, 5 mile Green Belt, 1m
       to be housed in overspill New Towns
       — plus Distribution of Industry Act (many
       loopholes) —→ 1947 Town and Country
       Planning Act: limited dev. of inner London
       - 'nationalized right to develop land' (Hall)
       1949 National Parks and Access to Countryside
       Act: rec. areas and rights of public to
       countryside

   (b) Extent of change
       i) Migration: 1946-50 — 14 NTs (Eng and Wales) and London
          overspills
          By 1971 — 29 NTs, pop of 1m
          but   inter-regional mig. to L and South till 1966

       ii) Reconstruction: 1950s major slum clearance & reconstruction
           programs (inc. high-rise)←shortage of
           land

       iii) Transport: 1950s — L 'worst congested'(Hall) road system
            in world — commuting from NTs —→ motorways,
            multi-storey carparks.

BUT 3. Neglect of social objectives and quality of life

   (a) high rise dev./displacement of low income from housing
       with no adequate replacement. Urban decay. High income
       to peripheral suburbs
   (b) quality of services (education, transport) and physical
       environ. (air, water) deteriorating in inner urban areas
   (c) employment: dislocation?

Conclusion: Improvements at macro level in physical structure but
            need to plan for social objectives only realized with
            hindsignt.

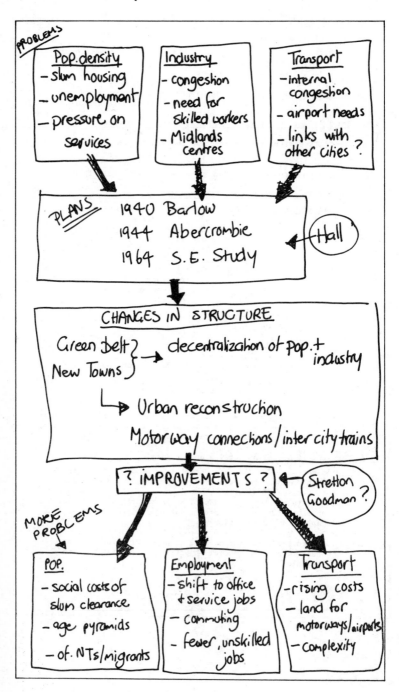

PROBLEMS

Pop. density
- slum housing
- unemployment
- pressure on services

Industry
- congestion
- need for skilled workers
- Midlands centres

Transport
- internal congestion
- airport needs
- links with other cities ?

PLANS   1940 Barlow
        1944 Abercrombie
        1964 S.E. Study   ← Hall

CHANGES IN STRUCTURE

Green belt ?
New Towns } → decentralization of pop. + industry

        ↳ Urban reconstruction
        Motorway connections / inter city trains

? IMPROVEMENTS ?   ← Stretton Goodman ?

MORE PROBLEMS

POP.
- social costs of slum clearance
- age pyramids
- of. NTs/migrants

Employment
- shift to office + service jobs
- commuting
- fewer, unskilled jobs

Transport
- rising costs
- land for motorways/airports
- complexity

A third student, Edward, produced the quite different approach shown opposite.

If you compare these plans for the same essay, you may find that one system appeals more strongly to your own style of working. Or that you have developed an individual system of planning which suits you. You may even agree with David, the student in Chapter 5, who starts writing *in order* to clarify his argument. Whatever the case, the important point is that there is no one way that suits everyone and that is clearly superior on all occasions.

All of these students were awarded credits for the essays they finally wrote.

Appendix 6

Reorganization of the first draft: an example (see Chapter 6, page 65)

Here are the stages a student went through in reorganizing a first-year Sociology essay.

Topic: Drawing on personal experience of ceremonies (marriage, funerals, graduations, prize-giving, etc.), discuss the extent to which Garfinkel's criteria apply to all ceremonies involving status alteration. (Text: *H. Garfinkel*, 'Conditions of successful degradation ceremonies'.)

First draft: 'Conditions of successful degradation ceremonies', an article by Harold Garfinkel, indicates a specific form of the rites of passage; that is a manner through which an individual undergoes a change in status using a ceremony to mark the occasion. Garfinkel's criteria apply to some changes of status whether positive or negative but cannot be used to describe all status changes.

Garfinkel's article states that the degradation ceremony is made up of several points. The first is the ritual separation and ostracising of the individual (known as the perpetrator), the second is the ceremony in which he (the perpetrator) has status removed (in front of witnesses) and emerges a degraded individual.

A most notable degradation ceremony (and one to which Garfinkel's ideas can be applied) occurs when an army officer is publicly stripped of his commission. The officer is set apart from his peers, ostracised and noted as a deviant from army norms. He is then taken to a ceremony presided over by a notable army personage (in whom the army vests its authority); during this ceremony, the officer is stripped of his rank. *However*, another more common occurrence of degradation which cannot be applied to Garfinkel's criteria is that of an unwed mother. Society denounces an unwed mother and ostracises her throughout her pregnancy but doesn't set her apart from society though a stigma is attached to the child's illegitimacy. There is no ceremony to mark this change of status but society sees the mother's actions as a threat to its codes.

Some positive changes in status conform to Garfinkel's criteria; one of these is Christian marriage. The wedding date is announced and the couple involved are ritually separated from society and each other and are brought together in the church. The bride walks down the aisle on her father's left—an inferior position—the couple is separated from the congregation (witnesses) and from the priest who officiates at the wedding. The priest is recognised as an upholder of Christian society's morals. The man and the woman are ceremonially united as one entity and they both emerge married and the woman (generally) takes the husband's name. Another status change which conforms to Garfinkel's ideas is that of a graduation ceremony. The student is also set aside from society and walks down a corridor to the ceremony. The ceremony (at university graduations) is conducted by the Vice-Chancellor. He confers the degree on the student in front of many witnesses and the student then emerges with a degree. *But* Garfinkel's criteria do not wholly apply to a coming-out ceremony in the Trobriand Islands. The ceremony occurs three months after childbirth when a mother who has been segregated from the rest of the village comes back into society. The ceremony is only celebrated by the family and a few close friends with no apparent master or mistress of ceremonies. The mother comes out dressed in traditional garb with betelnut makeup and head-dress to denote the occasion. The woman then assumes the role of motherhood and increased status involved with childbirth.

Garfinkel's article stating the events of degradation can also be applied to gradation ceremonies. However, its use is limited as many gradation and degradation ceremonies do not follow the same format.

As it stands, the flow of thought is somewhat difficult to follow. This is because the paragraphing is haphazard. Remember those general insights about the paragraph we discussed in Chapter 3? That the paragraph is the basic unit of thought? That statements within one paragraph should cohere around one basic idea? That it is often a useful technique to lead with the main idea at the head of the paragraph? Now look at the organization of paragraphs in this first draft:

Paragraph 1: Explanation of Garfinkel's theory of degradation ceremonies, and the qualification that the term cannot be used to describe all status changes.

Paragraph 2: Analysis of the structure of a degradation ceremony.
Examples: (1) demotion of an army officer — meets Garfinkel's criteria.

Paragraph 3: *However* (2) society's treatment of an unwed mother — does not meet criteria.

Paragraph 4: Examples (3) marriage and (4) graduation are positive examples of status change ceremonies — these meet Garfinkel's criteria.
But (5) criteria only partly applicable to a Trobriand coming-out ceremony.

Paragraph 5: Garfinkel's criteria cannot be applied to all ceremonies involving status alteration.

In this draft the student had attempted to get down in words both a summary of the basic concept being examined and a variety of examples to which this concept could be applied. But how far is the present arrangement of material in paragraph units effective? What is the effect on the reader of the two longer paragraphs in the middle of the essay by comparison with the much shorter ones at the beginning and end? Are the examples arranged in the order which most effectively develops the argument that Garfinkel's criteria are not universally applicable? Are there significant shifts in the thinking in paras 3 and 4, indicated by the contrast-setting terms *however* and *but*? (These words were not in italics in the original draft).

This student, following a group discussion, revised her essay according to the following structure.

Paragraph 1: A combination of the original paragraphs 1 and 2, focused on Garfinkel's theory and criteria.

Paragraph 2: Analysis of examples 1, 3 and 4 which all meet Garfinkel's criteria and which include both positive and negative changes in status.

Paragraph 3: Analysis of examples 2 and 5 which do not meet all the criteria and are examples of contrasting change in status following childbirth.

Paragraph 4: Conclusion.

She still had to do more revision on the actual wording and style of the essay and to clarify the opening sentences of each paragraph. In general, however, the restructuring of the material at the paragraph level was the major achievement of the redrafting stage. The essay is now more logically structured and better balanced.

Appendix 7

Introductions: further examples
(see Chapter 6, page 70)

Here are two introductions to the same essay topic in an
English Literature course.

Topic: A novelist has many possible ways of letting the reader
know what a character is 'like': straight-forward narrative commentary, for example, or first-person narration in which the
character tells his or her thoughts, concerns, feelings. In most
familiar forms of drama, however, a character must be portrayed
only externally and indirectly through dialogue, appearance and
action. Discuss Ibsen's characterisation of Hedda Gabler, paying
particular attention to specific ways in which he attempts to
show the audience what sort of a person Hedda is.

Example 1
In Hedda Gabler Hedda is portrayed by Ibsen externally and
indirectly. Hedda's mind is not deeply explored by Ibsen, so that
we, the audience, are invited to reconstruct her character from
her utterances, her situation and her actions. Specifically, Ibsen
attempts to show the audience Hedda's character through comments on her by other characters and by Hedda's conversations
with the others. One can also learn about Hedda's character
through her reactions to her present situation and her attachment
to her past.

Example 2
Hedda Gabler is a play with a central personality initiating the
action, and seemingly in control. Hedda, the central character,
sets up the action; for example, she is the one to get Tesman to
write to Lovborg (p. 282), giving her the opportunity to cross-
examine Mrs Elvsted. Hedda is also the instigator in Lovborg's
demise of character and his subsequent death (p. 308).

Example 1 sets out systematically both the writer's point of
view about the topic (Hedda is presented 'externally and

indirectly') and the areas through which the writer will move in order to establish the validity of that point of view. Though the paragraph is far from perfect in style, the writer has achieved her purpose.

Now look again at the topic and Example 2. Is Example 2 an effective opening? Is it well focused on the topic? On the basis of those two openings, which essay seems more likely to meet the demands of the topic?

Appendix 8

Introduction: process of redrafting (see Chapter 6, page 72)

Here are three stages one student went through in trying to clarify the ideas in her introduction.

Topic: How effective a President was George Washington? What were his main contributions to the office of the Presidency? What was his view of the Constitution?

1st attempt
George Washington was not a terribly brilliant man but was extremely ambitious. In his younger years, Washington was a grand manager of his own affairs and that of the first government of America.

His ambition in early life led him to be an officer in the Royal Army against the French. During the War of Independence he became America's 'nation-wide' hero after bringing the 'Yankees' to victory.

2nd attempt
Within the framework of the Constitution, George Washington created the role of the President of the United States of America. Washington's effectiveness as a president rested upon his views and interpretation of the Constitution. The office of the President was expressed on paper as an executive power, a commander in chief of the Army, Navy, and militia of the states as well as a treaty maker and an overall administrator. George Washington was not merely effective in carrying out these powers, but he gave the office importance and dignity which has since been associated with the U.S. Presidency.

(This draft continued without any paragraph breaks for two pages, as the student was primarily concerned at this stage with clarifying her ideas.)

3rd attempt
Within the framework of the Constitution of 1787, George Washington created the role of the President. Overall, Washington's effectiveness rested upon his activities as President which were modified by his views and interpretation of the Constitution. The President was defined by the Constitution as a holder of executive power, a commander-in-chief of the Army, Navy and militia of the state as well as a treaty maker and an administrator. George Washington was not merely effective in carrying out these duties but he gave the office the dignity and importance which have since been associated with the U.S. Presidency.

If you compare these three versions you may recognise the shifts through which this student's thinking has gone. Her first version is purely descriptive detail about George Washington and would be a poor introduction to an analytical essay. Her second version moves much more directly into analysing and pulling together the main strands of the set topic though, as yet, it has no clear shape. The third version, which could still be improved in style, is a much clearer attempt to place the significance of George Washington's contribution to the Presidency within an analytical framework which can be worked out in detail in the body of the essay.

Appendix 9

Features of academic style: an example (see Chapter 6, page 75)

Check if you can identify some of those features of academic style we discussed on p. 75. Read the following extract from a Sociology textbook in order to find answers to these questions:

- what sort of *approach* does the writer use?
- how would you describe the *tone* of this extract?
- can you pick out any of the features of grammar and vocabulary we listed on p. 78?

To get you started, let's examine the first sentence of the extract. What characteristic features of academic style can you notice?

Are not both psychology and sociology, then, it might be asked, equally concerned with the way individual behaviour is socially conditioned?

approach	a tentative debate, an invitation to more precise exploration, an appeal to reason.
tone	formal language (how would you ask this question in ordinary speech?), impersonal, a 'lofty' rhetorical question.
grammar & vocabulary	the clause 'it might be asked' is introduced by an *impersonal pronoun* (it) and uses a *passive* form of the verb (be asked); see too the verb 'is conditioned'.
	the use of this secondary clause makes the sentence structure *complex*.
	the word 'conditioned' is used in a more *specialised* sense here than in ordinary speech.

Read on now for yourself, trying as you go to pick out more of the same features of academic style.

Are not both psychology and sociology, then, it might be asked, equally concerned with the way individual behaviour is socially conditioned? The answer is 'Yes', but the psychologist's point of attention is usually the individual, the sociologist's that of the groups and categories to which the individual belongs. But that is to put it too crudely, for psychologists do study groups and categories, too: the attitudes, say, of miners, disc-jockeys, sadists, or women. The real difference is that the unit or frame of reference for the psychologist is the behaviour of the individual, whether his inner 'psyche' or its external manifestations observable in his relationships with others. The sociologist approaches perhaps exactly the same piece of behaviour 'from the other end', as it were, and asks what the significant regularities and patterns in a person's behaviour are that enable us to see him as typical of others who have been similarly socialized, undergone parallel life experiences, or belonged to similar groups. Social behaviour is thus not simply the putting together of all the separate 'natural' behaviours of many individuals — what is called 'aggregate psychology' — it is a qualitatively different *level* of behaviour, not 'given' in the *individual* psyche independently of its experience of society, as it were, but produced *in social groups* and internalized within the individual as a result of exposure to the pressures of these groups. Both the psychologist and the sociologist, then, may study the same behaviour and ask similar questions. It is not, crudely, that one studies the group and the other the individual, but the focus or 'point of entry' will be the individual for the psychologist, and for the sociologist the society and culture of which the individual is a part. They will thus frequently converge in their studies, and at the borderlines it becomes rather arbitrary whether one labels a study 'psychology' or 'sociology'. Yet the psychologist, basically, is interested in the way the individual's behaviour is organized so as to constitute a 'personality', the sociologist in the way the individual as a person relates to others.

The differences between sociology and psychology, on the one hand then, are differences of *perspective*, in the same way as the differences between a sociologically minded historian and an 'empiricist' historian are differences of perspective. The differences between law, political science and economics, on the other hand, are differences of what one might term *domain*, in that each has a prime interest in certain substantive areas only within human behaviour in general, that is, the lawyer in the study of the way men resolve 'trouble issues', the economist in the study of production and consumption. Of course, at the widest, the lawyer who looks at the connection of law-making agencies to the rest of society, or who studies how different kinds of behaviour become defined as 'good' or 'bad' and how these definitions become embodied in law, is studying law in very sociological ways.

Researches within any one specific discipline may be vital to another: thus the sociologist may draw upon the economist's knowledge of the female labour-market as a part of his study of the family; conversely, the economist may use the sociologist's national surveys or local, intensive studies in order to enable him to estimate where and when likely supplies of labour, or demand for commodities, can be expected.

From P. Worsely (ed.) (1970), Introducing Sociology, 2nd edn, Penguin, pp. 33–4.

Appendix 10

Writing a book review
(see Chapter 9, page 96)

1 Here are two examples of instructions given by lecturers for book review assignments. Notice how the questions shape the structure that the review should take.

Book review in Political Economy (1500 words)

The review should not be a summary of the book. Instead it should state what the book sets out to do and assess how well the author achieves that goal. Your review might be *guided* by the following questions:

Objectives:	What does the book set out to do?
Theory:	Is there an explicit theoretical framework? If not, are there important theoretical assumptions?
Concepts:	What are the central concepts? Are they clearly defined?
Argument:	What is the central argument? Are there specific hypotheses?
Method:	What methods are employed to test these?
Evidence:	Is evidence provided? How adequate is it?
Values:	Are value positions clear or are they implicit?
Literature:	How does the work fit into the wider literature?
Contribution:	How well does the work advance our knowledge of the subject?
Style:	How clear is the author's language/style/expression?
Conclusion:	What brief overall assessment is possible?

Book review in Women's Studies (1500 words)

I would like all students to produce a short critical book review...

Some questions to ask yourself:

Who am I writing for?
What shared knowledge and values am I assuming?

Why does any of this matter?
Why should anyone believe me?
What are my reasons for thinking the way I do?
What is my evidence?

Formal qualities I shall look for include:

a. evidence of understanding the book's basic terminology and argument
b. conceptual clarity
c. consistent and logical argument supported by evidence
d. independent judgement

Content should include:

a. a summary of the book's scope and argument
b. an assessment of the book in its own terms (i.e. how well does it do what it sets out to do?)
c. an assessment of the book in your own terms (e.g. is the topic worthwhile? does the book deal with the topic in the best way? how could it be improved?)

2 Here is a suggested checklist for the final draft of your book review. Note that the questions in this checklist relate directly to the suggested structure of the book review set out in Step 4 of *Writing the Review* in Chapter 9.

1. Have I identified the book clearly, right at the start?

2. Is the author's argument clearly and objectively summarised so that my reader can recognize the theoretical approach and the range of material covered? (about a third of a short review).

3. Have I clearly identified and discussed the 2–3 key issues I wish to raise in relation to this book? (about 50% of the review)

4. Have I given reasons for my criticisms and my approval of different aspects of the book?

5. Is there a final evaluation of the book's importance, based on my previous discussion?

Appendix 11

Checklist for a Psychology lab report (see Chapter 9, page 99)

Here is a detailed checklist for a Psychology lab report made up by a lecturer for her first year class. It may give you some idea of the detailed expectations about the content, style and format of such a report.

1. **Title:** does it indicate   topic area?
    purpose of experiment?
    direction of hypothesis?

2. **Abstract:**   necessary? length? full sentences?
self-contained?
does it cover each section of the report:
    Intro (problem/hypothesis), i.e. purpose?
    Methods (minimal relevant information),
    i.e. how experiment was done?
    Results (significant data), i.e. findings?
    Discussion (conclusions re hypothesis),
    i.e. implications?

3. **Introduction:** does it make clear   topic of research
interest:
    importance?
    definitions?

  previous research
findings:
    chronological?
    grouped by
    research focus/
    methodology?
    logical sequence
    in presentation?

  gaps? weaknesses?
area for extension?

(leading to)   purpose of your experiment?

<u>does it state your hypothesis (or aim) clearly in final paragraph?</u>

(The Introduction section is presented in paragraphs, and previous research is briefly summarised rather than directly quoted. It should <u>persuade</u> your reader that your experiment has value and that <u>your hypothesis</u> is reasonable to explore.)

4. **Method:** check   order of sub-headings?

                coverage of <u>all</u> information necessary for replication?

                <u>only</u> information necessary for replication?

                logical sequence of description of procedure?

                reference to Appendices for complex information?

(The Method section is always written in the past tense. The amount of detailed explanation of sample selection, design, apparatus, procedures, etc will depend on how relevant these factors are to your final discussion.)

5. **Results:** tables, figures, etc: adequate title?

                          units of measurement clearly indicated?

                          statistical analysis identified?

                          relevant findings only?

          text: does it: direct attention to findings relevant to hypothesis?

                          indicate relative importance of various findings?

                          prepare reader for Discussion section to follow?

                          refer to each table/figure in order?

                is it: objective?

                        self-contained?

(The Results section should be precise, succinct, crystal clear, and <u>not</u> evaluative.)

6. **Discussion:** does it   <u>start by referring findings to hypothesis?</u>

                      discuss individual findings in relation to research cited in Introduction?

if findings are unexpected/do not support hypothesis/conflict with previous research, does it indicate:

possible sources of error:
hypothesis?
sample size/composition?
materials?
methods?
classification of results?
variations for subsequent experiments?

(The Discussion section is presented in paragraphs. It should direct your reader's attention to those aspects of the experiment which were successful in terms of your stated aim and hypothesis (and suggest the next step that might be taken), and those which were unsuccessful in terms of your hypothesis and previous research (and suggest variations in design, etc).)

7. **References:**   correct format?
all the sources referred to in report?
only the sources referred to in report?
absolutely accurate?

8. **Appendices:**   clearly titled?
raw data?
complex methodology (questionnaires, scoring schedules, etc)?
statistical analysis?

For **Final editing** check: spelling, especially names, terms, capital letters
grammatical sentences
paragraph units
headings/sub-headings
references in text/final References
tables, especially titles and numbers
format requirements (cover sheet, margins, spacing, etc)

Appendix 12

Suggested reference books and supplementary materials (see Chapter 7, page 83)

General reference works

Concise Oxford Dictionary (Clarendon Press, Oxford, 1976) or Longman Concise English Dictionary (Longman, Essex, 1989) are probably the best choices for a portable dictionary. For more intensive dictionary work, use the two-volume Shorter Oxford English Dictionary. For students whose first language is not English, the most comprehensive and clearly presented dictionary is A.S. Hornby's Oxford Advanced Learner's Dictionary of Current English (Oxford University Press, Oxford, 1974).

Roget's Thesaurus (Penguin, London, 1970) is useful for helping you find the exact word.

The M.H.R.A. Style Book, 2nd edn (Modern Humanities Research Association, London, 1978) is frequently used in Britain by authors.

The M.L.A. Style Sheet, 2nd edn (Mod. Lang. Ass. Amer., New York, 1970) is a standard reference manual for American and British academic writing.

Oxford Dictionary for Writers and Editors (Clarendon Press, Oxford, 1981) is a comprehensive guide to spelling of unusual words.

K.L. Turabian, A Manual for Writers of Term Papers, Theses and Dissertations, 4th edn (University of Chicago Press, Chicago, 1973) is a standard American manual with exhaustive models of referencing format.

Aids to editing

In addition to the M.H.R.A. Style Book and the M.L.A. Style Sheet, which are the most comprehensive texts, the following more specialised books should also be helpful.

On punctuation:
    G.V. Carey (1958), Mind the Stop, rev. edn, Penguin, London.
    E. Partridge (1964), You have a Point There, Hamish Hamilton, London.

On grammar (traditional English grammar):
    R. Quirk & S. Greenbaum (1973), University Grammar of English, Longman, London.

On grammar for students whose first language is not English:
    A.S. Hornby (1975), Guide to Patterns and Usage in English, 2nd edn, Oxford University Press, Oxford.

Style and usage

Three standard works on usage and correctness are:
    H.W. Fowler (1965), A Dictionary of Modern English Usage, 2nd edn rev. by Sir E. Gowers, Clarendon Press, Oxford.
    Sir E. Gowers (1962), The Complete Plain Words, Penguin, London.
    E. Partridge (1963), Usage and Abusage, Penguin, London.

On style, there are two entertaining and instructive works, well stocked with examples:
    R. Graves & A. Hodge (1965), The Reader Over Your Shoulder, Cape, London.
    F.L. Lucas (1974), Style, Cassell, London.

For Science students wanting a comprehensive text on lab reports, articles and theses, a good current guide is:

    D. Lindsay (1984), A Guide to Scientific Writing, Longman Cheshire, Melbourne.

Finally the best hour's worth of reading on style is probably Orwell's famous essay:

G. Orwell, 'Politics and the English Language' available in Inside the Whale and Other Essays, Penguin, London, 1966, and in most collected editions of Orwell.

Appendix 13

Direct quotations
(see Chapter 7, page 85)

Whenever you use a direct quotation in an essay there are certain formalities which must be observed:

1 You must copy *exactly* the wording of the original text. If, for reasons of comprehension or grammatical coherence, additions or omissions are essential, then there are recognised procedures for handling this (see below).

2 Every direct quotation must be followed by a full *reference* to the source you took it from, including the precise page number(s) where the passage occurred. (See Appendix 14 for details of referencing styles.)

3 Any printed materials from which you quote must be included in your *bibliography*. (See Appendix 15 for details on bibliography.)

If these conventions are not observed in your essay, you may be accused of *plagiarism*, which is the academic sin of claiming the words and works of others as your own.

Format

When you include quotations in your essay, you should follow these general guidelines for format:

1 If the quotation takes up less than three lines in *your* handwritten or typed essay, then include it in the body of the essay and enclose it in quotation marks (either single or double).

2 If the quotations takes up *more than three lines*, then indent the whole quotation (that is, make the margin wider) and, if you are typing, use single-spacing. Quotation marks should *not* be used with this format.

Look at the following extract from an Economic History essay and note the format used for the quotations:

> Moreover, the influence of culture upon economic expectations and consumption choices is important. Douglas and Isherwood (1980, p. 58) point out:
>
> > In most cultures reported over the world, there are certain things that cannot be sold or bought. One obvious case with us is political advance (which should not be bought); as to selling, a man who is capable of selling his honor, or even of selling his grandmother, is condemned by cliché.
>
> The investigation of cultural variables is termed 'social accounting'. It takes for granted that 'reality is socially constructed and also...that reality can be analysed as logical structures in use' (Douglas & Isherwood, 1980, p. 64) and focuses on interpretation of the economic evidence and procedures which operate <u>within</u> a specific cultural group.

Special punctuation marks in direct quotations

1 When quoting a passage, if you *alter* or *add* anything to the exact words used by the original writer, you must indicate these changes by *square brackets*, thus [ ]. Such changes may be necessary in order to:

- *add essential explanatory information*; for example, a passage from a Linguistics essay:

> Whorf has argued that different languages dissect time differently. For example, Hopi is said by Whorf to be a 'timeless' language in which the verb does not distinguish between past, present and future. Yet he also admits that the Western concept of dimensional time can be approximated in Hopi by other linguistic means:
>
> > It [Hopi grammar], by means of its forms called aspects and modes, also makes it easy to distinguish among momentary, continued and repeated occurrences, and to indicate the actual sequence of reported events. (3)
>
> So in this case language is not a true determinant of cultural experience but merely a reflection of a cultural tendency.

- integrate the quotation into the *grammatical structure* of the essay; for example, a passage from a Political Science essay:

  > The policies of the Conservative Party, under Douglas-Home and Heath, had become 'progressively less attractive to both the workers in industry and to the multi-national companies [which were] extending their European markets'. (7)

- include a comment or indication of your own *opinion* about the material you are quoting, or to indicate an *error* (in which case you use the Latin 'sic', meaning 'thus', enclosed in square brackets). For example, a passage from a History essay:

  > According to Senator Cristiano Otoni, speaking to the Brazilian Upper Chamber in 1883, before the end of the slave trade, owners had been 'careless as to the duration of the life [sic] of their slaves'.

Here the student uses [sic] to indicate a grammatical error — 'life' instead of 'lives' — in the original text.

2 If you *leave out* words from a complete sentence in the original source, you indicate this omission by three spaced dots, thus . . .

Such omissions may be made:

- at the *beginning* or *end* of a passage, either in order to adjust the quotation to the grammar of your sentence or to omit less relevant material. However, if the quotation is clearly a syntactic fragment (only part of a longer sentence but clear in meaning in itself), then it is not essential to indicate omissions, especially at the beginning of the quotation. For example, a passage from an Anthropology essay, where the omission of words from the direct quotations is not indicated as it occurs at the *start* of the original sentence:

  > Literacy also 'equips people to perform the varied tasks required in the modernizing society' (Lerner, 1958: 60) and 'spreads the consumption of urban products beyond the city limits' (Lerner, 1958: 61).

Here is a passage from a Sociology essay where the omission of words from the quotation *is* indicated since it occurs at the *end* of the original sentence:

> Turning now to the sociological components of the study, it is firstly necessary to define what is sociological. 'Sociologists use

the scientific method to learn how human groups are put together and how they function...' (Mack & Young, 1968: 1)

- in the *centre* of a quotation, where certain phrases or clauses are not relevant to the point being made in your essay. In such cases the omission must *always* be indicated. For example, a passage from a Prehistory essay:

  > However, while it can be relatively easy to recognize patterns of behaviour and 'to infer from them some of the parameters of the activities which produced them,... it is much more difficult to determine the nature of the social unit which performed those activities' (Freeman, 1968, p. 265).

Appendix 14

References (see Chapter 7, page 85)

In an academic essay whenever you are:

- quoting the exact words of another writer,
- closely summarising a passage from another writer,
- using an idea or material which is directly based on the work of another writer,

then you must identify and acknowledge your source in a systematic style of referencing. Otherwise you may be accused of *plagiarism* (see Appendix 13).

The three most common styles for references to printed materials are footnotes, endnotes, and included references. Different departments within a university may favour different styles, so it is essential that you check on the preferred format for each course in which you are studying. Essays in literary criticism, for example, in which frequent reference is made to the same literary text have their own characteristic style of citation.

In general your aim must be to include in your reference all the information that is necessary for your reader to trace the source of your material easily and accurately.

Footnotes and endnotes

The first two systems of referencing, footnotes and endnotes, are very similar: in both, you insert a number (either in brackets or slightly above the line) in your text at the end of a sentence or immediately following a direct quotation. For footnotes these numbers may either run consecutively through the whole essay or start afresh with (1) at the start of each new page; for endnotes the numbering is always consecutive. With footnotes the information about the source of each numbered reference is given at the bottom of each page of your text; with endnotes the same information is given in a consolidated list at the end of the essay.

Format: The following points should be noted, both for use in your own essays and to enable you to interpret the footnotes and endnotes you encounter in your reading:

1 On a *first citation* of a work, full details, as in the bibliography, must be given, together with a *precise page reference*; for example, 'R. Beard (1970), <u>Teaching and Learning in Higher Education</u>, Penguin, London,' p. 49.'

2 *Subsequent references* to the same work may be cited by:

• *short form*: the writer's name, the short title, and the page number;
  e.g. Beard, <u>Teaching and Learning</u>, pp. 89–91.
• op. cit.: (i.e. *opere citato*, Latin, 'in the work cited') This is <u>used</u> following the writer's name and followed by the page reference when the citation is to the same work referred to earlier but not in the immediately preceding footnote. It should be underlined.
  e.g. 1 M. Douglas (1973), <u>Natural Symbols</u>, Penguin, London, p. 88.
      2 R. Fox (1967), <u>Kinship and Marriage</u>, Penguin, London, p. 161
      3 M. Douglas, op. cit., p. 132.
• ibid.: (i.e. *ibidem*, Latin, 'in the same place') This is used, with a following page number, when the citation is to the same work referred to in the immediately preceding footnote. It should be underlined,
  e.g. 1 M. Douglas (1973), <u>Natural Symbols</u>, Penguin, London, p. 68
      2 <u>ibid.</u>, pp. 70–1
      3 <u>ibid.</u>, p. 173

3 *Other common abbreviations* in references:

• <u>loc. cit.</u> (*loco citato*, 'in the place already quoted') has confused usage (and you would probably be wise to avoid it in your own writing). It is sometimes used in place of <u>op. cit.</u> when the reference is to an article or chapter rather than a book. It is sometimes used in place of <u>ibid.</u> when the citation is to the same source and the same page as the immediately preceding reference. It is sometimes used in place of <u>op. cit.</u> when the citation is to the same page as the previous citation on the same source.

- f. (or ff.) ('and the following page(s)') is used to indicate frequent references to an item within a few consecutive pages.
  e.g. R. Fox, <u>Kinship and Marriage</u>, p. 71f.

- passim ('scatteredly') is used when the reference is to items to be found throughout that source or that section of a book.
  e.g. Beard, <u>Teaching and Learning</u>, passim.

4 *Complex references:* If you are citing a quotation or material which you have found already quoted by another writer, include in your citation both the full bibliographic details of the original quotation (which you will find in the reference) and the details of the book in which you found it. e.g. H. Cox (1968), <u>The Secular City</u>, Penguin, London, p. 93, quoted in M. Douglas (1973), <u>Natural Symbols</u>, Penguin, London, p. 37.

Included references

In this third style of referencing, which is commonly used in Science and the Social Sciences, all references are cited in the body of your text. The references are extremely brief (writer's name, date of publication, page number) and the full bibliographic information is supplied in the bibliography.

Format:

1 If the writer's name appears in the text of your essay, the remaining items of the citation will follow this in brackets.

> e.g. Beard (1970; pp. 91–2) argues that concept learning is important.

(Here the actual argument is found on pages 91 and 92.)

> e.g. Fox (1967) demonstrates the close relationship between kinship and marriage in certain societies.

(As this relationship is the theme of the whole book, no specific page references are given.)

2 If the writer's name does not appear in the text of your essay, the reference must include his or her name within the brackets and should come at the end of a sentence or immediately following a direct quotation.

e.g. It has been argued that concept learning is important (Beard, 1970, p. 91–2).

Comparison of referencing styles

Each style of referencing has characteristic advantages:

1 Footnotes make it easy for the reader to identify a source immediately merely by glancing to the bottom of the page. However, lengthy footnotes, including comments and additional information, can be distracting and clumsy.

2 Endnotes permit extended commentary and additional information, but require the reader to refer constantly between the actual text and the final pages of the essay.

3 Included references are extremely efficient but can only identify a source and allow no room for additional comments.

In order to demonstrate these styles of referencing more clearly, we have taken a passage from a student's Prehistory essay and used included references in Version 1 and footnotes in Version 2. Endnotes would follow the Version 2 style, except that the citations for the whole essay would be listed at the end.

Version 1
The work of van Lawick-Goodall (1971), Kortlandt and van Zon (1968), and Wright (1972) shows that present-day chimpanzees, orangutans and macaque monkeys are capable of using simple tools and bipedal locomotion. Wright (1972, p. 305) concluded, after tool-using experiments with a captive orangutan, that manipulative disability is not a factor which would have prevented Australopithecines from mastering the fundamentals of tool technology. However, while there is an unquestionable validity in comparing the behaviour of present-day apes with early hominids, it is important to note, as Howells (1973, p. 53) says, 'a Pantroglodyte is not and cannot be the ancestor of man. He cannot be an ancestor of anything but future chimpanzees.'

However, van Lawick-Goodall (1971, p. 233) suggests that the modern chimpanzee shows a type of intelligence closer to that of man than is found in any other present-day mammal. She argues that

...the chimpanzee is, nevertheless, a creature of immense significance to the understanding of man... He has the ability to solve quite complex problems, he can use and make tools for a variety of purposes... Who knows what the chimpanzees will be like forty million years hence? (van Lawick-Goodall, 1971, pp. 244–245)

The bibliography following the essay from which this passage was taken includes the following items:

Howells, W. (1973), Evolution of the Genus Homo, Addison-Wesley Pub. Co.

Kortlandt, A. & van Zon, J.C.J. (1968), 'The present state of research on the dehumanization hypothesis of African ape evolution', Proc. 2nd Int. Congr. Primatol., Atlanta, pp. 10–13.

van Lawick-Goodall, J. (1971), In the Shadow of Man, Collins.

Wright, R.V.S. (1972), 'Imitative learning of a flaked stone technology', Mankind 8, pp. 296–306.

Version 2

The work of van Lawick-Goodall,[1] Kortlandt and van Zon,[2] and Wright[3] shows that present-day chimpanzees, orangutans and macaque monkeys are capable of using simple tools and bipedal locomotion. Wright concluded, after tool-using experiments with a captive orangutan, that manipulative disability is not a factor which would have prevented Australopithecines from mastering the fundamentals of tool technology.[4] However, while there is unquestionable validity in comparing the behaviour of present-day apes with early hominids, it is important to note, as Howells says, 'a Pantroglodyte is not and cannot be the ancestor of man. He cannot be an ancestor of anything but future chimpanzees.'[5]

However, van Lawick-Goodall suggests that the modern chimpanzee shows a type of intelligence closer to that of man than is found in any other present-day mammal.[6] She argues that

...the chimpanzee is, nevertheless, a creature of immense significance to the understanding of man... He has the ability to solve quite complex problems, he can use and make tools for a variety of purposes... Who knows what the chimpanzees will be like forty million years hence?[7]

---

1 J. van Lawick-Goodall (1971), In the Shadow of Man, Collins.
2 A. Kortlandt & J.C.J. van Zon (1968), 'The present state of research on the dehumanization hypothesis of African ape evolution', Proc. 2nd Int. Congr. Primatol., Atlanta, pp. 10–13.
3 R.V.S. Wright (1972), 'Imitative learning of a flaked stone technology', Mankind 8, pp. 296–306.
4 ibid., p. 305.
5 W. Howells (1973), Evolution of the Genus Homo, Addison-Wesley Pub. Co., p. 53.
6 van Lawick-Goodall, op. cit., p. 233.
7 ibid., pp. 244–245.

Appendix 15

Bibliography (see Chapter 7, page 86)

Following every academic written assignment you are required to give a bibliography. This is an alphabetical list of all the printed sources of material you have found useful while preparing to write the assignment.

The ordering of items and the format of your bibliography are important. The style required may vary slightly from one discipline to another, *so always check if there are any specific departmental instructions about the format which you must observe.* Otherwise you can follow the pattern of bibliography used in any textbook for the course.

Here is an example of a bibliography which observes common practice. It is followed by a commentary on the points to be noted in the format.

Bibliography

Birnbaum, N. (1953), 'Conflicting interpretations of the rise of capitalism: Marx and Weber', Br. J. Sociol., IV, pp. 125–41.

Encyclopaedia of the Social Sciences, Vol. 3, 1930, 'Capitalism'.

Hansard, 3 July 1959, cols. 1245–1247.

Robertson, H.M. (1959), 'A criticism of Max Weber and his school', in R.W. Green (ed.), Protestantism and Capitalism: The Weber Thesis and Its Critics, Boston, D.C. Health & Co., pp. 65–80.

Tawney, R.H. (1921), The Acquisitive Society, New York, Harcourt Brace.

_____ (1926), Religion and the Rise of Capitalism, London, Murray.

The Times, 25 November 1959.

Weber, M. (1976), The Protestant Ethic and the Spirit of Capitalism (tr. Parsons), London, Allen & Unwin (orig. Ger. edit. 1904–5).

Note the following points.

A   Organisation of list

1 All books, articles and other sources are listed in *alpha-*

betical order by surname of writer (or organisation producing the source, see first two items in the above bibliography for examples). If more than one book or article is listed for the same writer (see Tawney example), they are arranged by date of publication. If they are both published in the same year, refer to them as 1926a and 1926b.

The alphabetical arrangement is a clear method of organising material and corresponds with the organisation of card catalogues and the arrangement of books, within sections, on the library shelves.

2 Some departments require you to make *separate lists* for books and for articles and government documents, or for primary and secondary sources.

B   Books

1 The author's *surname* is followed by initials or first name (see Tawney example).

If you are referring to a chapter by a particular writer which is included in a larger book, list the chapter under the writer's name and follow this with the full details of the editor's name, book title, etc. (see Robertson).

2 The *date* of publication must be included, either as the final item in the reference, or immediately following the writer's name as in this bibliography.

If you have used a recent edition or translation in your reading, give details of the edition you have used and add the date of the original edition in brackets (see Weber). The date is important in placing the source in a time context.

3 The *title* of the book is underlined (see Tawney). (This is what you look for as you run your eye along the library shelf.)

4 The title is followed by the *name of the publisher* and the *place of publication*. Some departments require only one or the other item. Be consistent in the pattern you follow and in the punctuation you use (see Tawney). (This information can be useful in establishing whether the book is written for an American or Australian audience.)

C   Articles

1 The *title* of the article or chapter is enclosed by quotation marks and followed by a comma. (Note: It is *not* underlined like the title of a book.)

2 The *name of the journal* (or book) is underlined. (This is what you look for on the library shelf.)

3 Full details of the journal are given, including (where relevant) the volume number, series number, date of issue, and the page references for the article cited (see Birnbaum).

D Government publications, newspapers, reference books, reports, etc.

1 Official publications are usually listed with the department or institution as the writer (see Hansard).

2 Standard reference books, such as encyclopaedias, are listed by their titles (see Encyclopaedia of the Social Sciences).

3 Newspaper items which are not signed are listed by the name of the newspaper (see The Times).

E Annotated bibliographies

Some departments require you to produce annotated bibliographies, that is, with a brief comment following each item which both summarizes the scope of the book or article and indicates in what way it was of particular significance to your purposes in writing your essay.

> Hart, C.M.W. and Pilling, A.R. (1960), The Tiwi of North Australia, Holt, Rinehart & Winston, New York.
>
> This is the standard monograph on the Tiwi comprising the earlier work of Hart on the ceremonies, social organization, economic system and daily life of this Aboriginal people, and the more recent description of the Tiwi in the 1950s by Pilling. It was particularly useful in providing an insight into the various forms of social control which operate in an island community.

Note: It is essential to head all the notes you take from printed materials with the full bibliographic information you might need if you later want to use material from the book or article in an essay or refer to the source in your own bibliography. Also remember to include page references for any major ideas or key quotations you include in your notes.